THE CHRI͟

# THE NEW FACE
# OF MISSIONS

Edgar R. Trexler

Publishing House
St. Louis London

Cover photo shows Queenstown Lutheran Church in Singapore. Some 35,000 people live in the apartments that surround the church and adjacent shopping center.

Concordia Publishing House, St. Louis, Missouri
Concordia Publishing House, Ltd., London, E. C. 1
Copyright © 1973 by Concordia Publishing House
*Library of Congress Catalog Card Number 72-97344*
*ISBN 0-570-06259-4*

MANUFACTURED IN THE UNITED STATES OF AMERICA

To
DAVID, MARK, and KAREN,
who will inherit
this new world

# CONTENTS

# INTRODUCTION

Recently some friends spent an evening at my home, looking at colored slides of Africa. They were enthralled by the lush greenery and the wild animals. But when the scenes turned to a modern city skyline and busy shops, you could feel the questions they were going to ask.

After the picture of a pretty young woman in a Western-style dress flashed on the screen, one man blurted, "She doesn't look like an African."

My friend was right. She didn't look like *his image* of an African. Her dress was stylish, and she stood in front of a cement block church. In a very real sense the comment revealed more about my friend than about the lady.

Like many North Americans, he had not realized how widely urban influences are taking hold in underdeveloped areas of the world. Although this does not imply urban affluence, it does mean that (1) church missions are facing a new sociological setting, and (2) churchgoers need a more realistic picture of the efforts they are supporting. The old images are out of date partly because changes are coming so rapidly. A more frightening reason is that too many church people are not concerned about things far from home.

For the last few years, I have spent a good deal of time reporting on missions in Southeast Asia, South America, and Africa. I have walked through stinking sewage paths in a Brazilian slum, bounced over rutty roads in what used to be called North Borneo, and sat on a zebra skin in a mud hut in Tanzania. But my major discovery has been that such scenes are a receding part of today's church missions picture.

These countries have also a heavy investment in a "new" world. And somehow I've been especially attracted to the side of church missions that is serving the new—the high-rise apartments, the industrial estates, the lay ministries and ecumenical ventures, the exciting church growth. Maybe these stories have appealed to me because they aren't well known. More likely it's because I've overcome some of my own misunderstandings.

I grew up in a pastor's home where my parents had an unusual interest in overseas missions. I remember well—and can show from my autograph book—nationals from overseas churches who visited in our home when I was a child. They came from Japan, India, Guyana, and elsewhere. Later I was a parish pastor and felt that I was fairly alert to the settings for missions abroad.

But one trip to mission areas—not to mention others that have come since—showed me that things weren't the way I had thought. It was a pleasant surprise, of course, to discover that I wasn't going to have to rough it. But more pleasant was the opportunity of seeing the incredibly impressive work that is being carried out in these new settings—work that, unfortunately, not enough people know about sufficiently or accurately. At this point my "pleasure" began disturbing me. I knew too many church people who were still clinging to such romantic notions as India lace and bare-breasted women, when in reality much of missions today deals with problems and joys similar to everyday American situations.

I've given many illustrations on the following pages from Africa, South America, and southern Asia because they collectively summarize the new setting for missions. They are also the areas of the most rapid growth of the church today. Underlying these selections is my conviction that God intended man for life in community with others.

The world is the scene for man's interaction with his fellowman—just as it is the scene for God's activity and dealings with men. This interaction, in which men cannot escape their responsibility for the world's condition and the course of human events, suggests that American church people do not have all the know-how about either the church or about living a life pleasing to God. For some difficult-to-fathom and basically selfish reasons, Americans often feel that they have the only answers to the world's questions and a stranglehold on wisdom.

Such is not the case. Our brothers have much to teach us. Laymen, for example, police chiefs, doctors, teachers, and other village leaders, are bringing about thousands of baptisms in Indonesia and Ethiopia. Another eye-opener is that because Christians are such a minority in some areas, they are fashioning remarkable cooperative ventures. In Singapore, Lutheran, Episcopal, Presbyterian, and Methodist seminarians study together in preparing for the ministry.

From nearly every part of the world come dramatic stories of church growth. The reasons are numerous: lay commitment, sociological factors, rising nationalism, evangelistic fervor—many of which could be examples for Americans struggling with waning church interest and influence. There is considerable need for Third World Christians to subject our American church life to the same searching critique which Western missionaries have vented on their countries and cultures. As we have done to them, they should do to us.

To sum up, world missions has an image problem. American church people have some myths to *un*learn and some lessons *to* learn from their brother-believers across the waters. Hopefully, this book will take a small step in that direction. If so, I am indebted to a host of people the world over—missionaries and citizens of many countries — who have taken me into their homes and confidences.

A large measure of gratitude also goes to John Mangum, secretary for planning for the Division for World Mission and Ecumenism of the Lutheran Church in America, who made many of those experiences possible; to my family, who with only a modest amount of complaining has been willing to see their husband/father away from home for chunks of time; and to my secretary, Mrs. Suzanne Tracy, who has struggled through many pages of my untidy manuscript.

To any who feel that the case is overstated on the following pages, I reply that we have a lot of overemphasis of the past to undo. To hold onto our old images of missions and to fail to see what we can learn from our friends abroad, is more than being shortsighted. It is being without integrity. God expects us to know our brothers deeply and sensitively, as Jesus knew us in the coming in the flesh. As Christians in our churches we are called to work together and share our learnings in alleviating man's condition and bringing about a world of hope. Our friends abroad deserve to be understood as they are, without implying that their development has escaped our notice. I hope they will bear with us until our images catch up with their reality.

EDGAR R. TREXLER

*Philadelphia, Pennsylvania*
*January 1973*

# Chapter 1

# THE WORLD GOES URBAN

The East Africa Airways jet makes its final approach to Dar es Salaam. The African countryside which appeared so green and lush from 30,000 feet gives way to the blue waters of the Indian Ocean and the skyline of the capital city of Tanzania. Suddenly, out one side of the plane, a section of the city comes into view which looks curiously like the suburban sprawl so typical of American cities.

Sure enough, there are a lot of houses, close together, alike in appearance, and fronting on gently winding roads. The roofs of the houses are made of zinc, the walls of cement blocks, and dozens of children are playing near them. The homes, I later learn, are middle-class housing in one of the city's new housing areas.

As I leave the airport there are other indications that the quiet seaport of Dar es Salaam (which means "haven of peace") is being transformed into a city of traffic jams, skyscrapers, and bustling stores. With its 335,000 population increasing by 10 percent each year, a million people will walk its streets in 20 years. By then, according to the city's master plan, Dar es Salaam will need 2,800 more hospital beds, 35 new clinics, 175 primary schools, 350 nursery schools, a civic college, a technical college, and 210 new churches.

Already the city points proudly to the expansive campus of the University of Tanzania. Classroom buildings, a snack bar, professors' offices, landscaped gardens, multistory dormitories, and an auditorium with a rounded dome like an American coliseum gleam in the African sunshine.

At a gas station up the street from my air-conditioned hotel, Volkswagens and other foreign cars fill up at 80 cents a British gallon. Behind the gas station is a motel and a dining room where $2 buys a rounded plate of fried shrimp and the best mug of iced tea that you've ever tasted.

Next is the New Africa Hotel, made famous by Ernest Hemingway. But only the front of the building and the sidewalk cafe remain. A new New Africa Hotel is going up. It will compare with the Kilimanjaro, now the largest hotel in town. Hemingway would be surprised at the rooftop discotheque at the Kilimanjaro and at the teletype machine in the lobby which bangs out the news of the world.

The next block is Independence Avenue where the red columns of the National Bank of Commerce are dominant. Airline offices stand side by side — East Africa Airways, KLM, Air India — their windows advertising trips to Hong Kong, Bangkok, and Athens. Around the corner is a hamburger shop named Wimpy's, with all the combinations of Kingburger, Wimpyburger, and Coca-Cola. A bookstore next door carries the current issues of *Time* and *Newsweek*, and a sign informs "Latest *Playboy* magazine received."

You have to remind yourself that this is Africa. For much too long the images of the dark and forbidding continent have blinded Americans from seeing that Africa is not all bush. But the realization that Africa is turning urban only accelerates the vision of the urbanization that is sweeping the whole world.

Nairobi, Kenya, has become East Africa's major jetport and starting place for vacations, safaris, and hunting expeditions. The circular Hilton Hotel in the center of the city is the equal of any hotel in the world. In Kampala, Uganda . . . Lagos, Nigeria . . . Accra, Ghana . . . the airport scene is the same. And so are sections of the cities.

A drive down a smooth street near the Atlantic Ocean

in the 100,000-population city of Monrovia, Liberia, takes you past the magnificent, golden Executive Mansion, the granite Supreme Court building with its statue of the blinded woman holding the scales of justice, and the box-like contours of the legislative building. Inland from Monrovia, Swedish, American, and German iron mines are causing population centers to spring up at Bomi Hills, Mano River, Nimba, and Bong Mine (the Nimba mine produces 10 million tons of ore a year). Rubber plantations at Firestone and Salala are having the same effect. About 25 percent of Liberia's one million population now lives in an urban/industrial environment, compared with 10 percent 10 years ago.

## High-rises and High Tension

I remember another day — this time not in Africa. The place is Singapore, with the shops jammed together. So are the people. Horns beep and bicyclists weave as people walk the streets and sidewalks. Singapore has 2 million people living on 224 square miles. The city has an old section, but it has a new part as well, and its modern shopping arcades and green plazas are sure signs of the new urban culture.

So are the high-rise apartment buildings. For 10 years Singapore has been building high-rises at the rate of 12,000 units per year. Gone are the thousands of squatters huts and palm-leaf houses that once dotted the downtown area. Today, one in every four Singaporeans lives in a flat, as the apartments are called. Because of immigration and a high birthrate (eight babies per hour in 1965), the government has erected more than 115,000 new units on 2,000 acres of the island nation. Rentals for the one-, two-, or three-room apartments are $6.65 (U. S.) per month per room.

"With no resources available and the population increase, the estates are a good answer to Singapore's problem," says Pastor John Nelson. "We think they're crowded, but the quality of life there is better than it was in the slums. There are no vacancies, and the list of waiting applicants is long. People who have lived with grandfather-father-and-son in one house are used to crowded conditions."

In the future even more dramatic changes are scheduled for the Singaporeans' way of life. The monorail is coming to speed people to and from work so that valuable land doesn't have to be consumed with freeways. Hovercraft that travel a few inches above the water on a cushion of air will speed people around the edges of the island.

*Anthills and Satellites*

If the traffic in Singapore is a problem, the situation is worse in Sao Paulo, Brazil. This city in southern Brazil is the sixth largest and the fastest growing metropolis in the world. At rush hour it is a human anthill of 6.3 million where Volkswagens clog the streets and sleek buildings shoot upwards. Sao Paulo even has satellite cities—four of them to be exact. Huge manufacturing plants for Ford, General Motors, Firestone, and Pirelli are located in these cities which are known locally as A, B, C, and D. Each initial, of course, stands for a name. *A*, for example, means Santo Andre.

Elsewhere in Brazil, the new capital city of Brasilia is an architectural masterpiece, a South American "new city" that rose out of the country's midsection where no town had previously existed. In the neighboring country to the north, Venezuela, the twin towers of the Simon Bolivar Civic Center are a striking centerpiece to downtown Caracas. The buildings shoot government offices 30 stories into the sky while multilaned Avenida Bolivar passes through the middle. At lunch time you can eat a hamburger in one of the shopping centers that mark Nelson Rockefeller's investments in the city.

These rapid changes gave rise to a recent magazine

article titled "Nothing Stays Nailed Down in South America Anymore." The text went on to talk about "the move to Marxism in Chile, the move to the extreme right in Brazil, the move to the city everywhere, and the move to a new self-image."

## The Urban Third World

These similar and surprising scenes come from three continents. If the descriptions had focused on cities like London, Copenhagen, Rome, Athens, or Jerusalem, you wouldn't have been so surprised. Nearly everyone is aware of the large cities of Western Europe and the Mediterranean. But the urban growth of the Third World countries — particularly Africa, sections of the Orient, and South America — has escaped the notice of most Americans.

Calcutta, India, for example, had 2,548,000 residents in 1941. Today the total is more than 5 million. Bombay had slightly less than 3 million inhabitants in 1941. Today it has 5.5 million. New Delhi jumped over a million in population in the last 30 years.

In the Far East urban growth is almost legendary. Hong Kong had 600,000 residents in 1945. It now has 4 million. Huge high-rise apartment buildings and double-decker buses greet the visitor. Grace Lutheran Church occupies a storefront like its neighboring shops. The view out the front door of the Hotel Astor includes a garish red and blue sign with the words, "Whisky Go-Go Bar" and a statue of a dancing girl in yellow shorts. If that isn't sufficiently enticing, signs for three other bars are within sight.

The spires of some government buildings in Kuala Lumpur, Malaysia, are reminiscent of those of the chapel of the Air Force Academy in Colorado. The airport terminal is a long, low building with graceful arches and wide walkways. The national mosque has a tower that rises high above the city. The University of Malaysia

15

has an expansive green campus with modern buildings at every turn.

Japan has become an affluent society – the big business man of Asia, with a gross national product second only to that of the United States. Cities are thriving and opulent. Highways are jammed with Japanese-built automobiles. Public transportation is the finest in the world. Americans are familiar with the urbanization of Japan through the goods that are available in local stores. Greater Tokyo, with 11 million residents, is the largest urban area in the world.

The island nation of Taiwan is also feeling the urban challenge. Migration into Taipei and other cities is creating a vacuum in the rural society, and the new urbanization is creating social and economic ills in cities unprepared to handle them.

Even unexpected places like Sabah, which I had known as North Borneo, are caught in the rush to urbanization. I've looked down from a mountaintop on the city of Kota Kinabalu and its 30,000 inhabitants. That came after enjoying the 1,000-mile champagne flight from Singapore to Sabah. An American school principal who lives in a hillside home that overlooks the sea invited me to dinner. The high school he oversees – and which is supported by the Lutheran Church in America – is a 3-story reinforced concrete building that compares favorably with any school in American suburbs. From time to time I sped along smooth roads in new cars, was escorted into air-conditioned government offices, and even met the president of the Basel Christian Church on the first tee of the Kinabalu Golf Club.

## Problems As Well as Potential

Becoming urban is not necessarily a blessing, particularly if the entire world is ultimately going to face the urban struggles America is undergoing. Consider the following brief news item:

SINGAPORE — Former Pennslvania Governor Raymond P. Shafer, Chairman of the U. S. Commission on Marijuana and Drug Abuse, arrived today to study a police crackdown on drug use among the young.

Singapore authorities are in the midst of one of the most intensive of their periodic purges of what they call the city's "drug culture." Some 32 rock musicians were arrested yesterday in one roundup.

It may be a fact of life that urbanization brings problems. This is not to say that rural life does not have problems, but advanced means of communication and transportation and the close proximity of people make urban problems more visible. And whether the country is America or elsewhere, the problems are similar.

New York City has had its crackdowns against prostitution. So has Hong Kong. America has its difficulties in solving clashes between racial and ethnic groups. So has Malaysia. Students in the United States have made their protests. So have those in Japan. Congested conditions between Washington and Boston are nerve-wracking. The same is true for Singapore.

Chew Loy Khoon of the Housing and Development Board of Singapore knows that the 10-story, 100-apartment, high-rise living quarters are better housing than the residents' old huts. But he understands when some people rebel against the heights and ask for lower floors. In the old huts, children could run and play where they wished. Now they're confined to a balcony or a general play area that serves a number of apartment buildings.

The close life creates tensions. "The whole island is a city," says one missionary. "All of life is intense and competitive. The challenge begins when you are born, and there's nowhere you can go to get away from it. There is little community spirit or pride among the renters."

In the country of Malaysia to the north, the race question that has plagued America in recent years raises its head. The only difference is the colorations. Constant agitation keeps the Malays, the Chinese, and the Indians at odds. The government, which is controlled by the Malays, is seeking to make "one nation, one language, one people" out of the country's diverse population. But the economic and commercial enterprises are largely in the hands of the Chinese. The ensuing struggle for power — political vs. commercial — brings distrust and intrigue.

Concerns of urban youth in Malaysia and Singapore would be recognizable to America's parents. The question is not long hair but the struggle for freedom. Chinese youth are not as self-disciplined as their parents, and they want more liberties than their elders enjoyed when they were young. "Times have changed," the youth say, but their parents fail to agree.

Young people quarrel with their parents over standards of morality ("Why should I go to church? If I don't steal or kill, I'm okay. The important thing is to get your own pleasure and not quarrel with others"). They argue over which girls to marry and what jobs to accept. Local observers tell stories of youngsters involved in secret societies, extortion rings, and gambling.

The youth hate their outmoded educational system where the emphasis is placed on memorization and passing examinations rather than on analyzing and understanding. At the conclusion of grades six, nine, and eleven, standardized exams (from Cambridge, England!) have to be passed. If you fail, your education is over. And so is your future.

The same frustrating system is used in Tanzania. The only difference is that if you live in a rural area and pass the sixth-grade exam, you have to go live in a city so you can attend junior high school. Sometimes the nearest school is 75 miles from a teen-ager's home, and he has to live in the city with a relative — or fend for himself, which breeds juvenile delinquency.

Mkiwa was a "street" boy, as they are called in Dar es Salaam. His very name means "friendless one." At one time he stayed with an aunt and slept in a lean-to near her house. When he got hungry, he stole. Finally he entered a boy's home operated by Lutheran Social Services, returned to school, was kicked out once for fighting, but finally calmed down to finish near the top of the class. Lutheran Social Service regularly assists over 100 such boys of junior high school age.

Urban poverty becomes an unhappy fact for thousands of rural poor who migrate to cities such as Caracas, Venezuela; or Rio de Janiero, Brazil; in search of employment and opportunity. Most get mired in the *barrios* and *favelas* where they own no land, pay no rent, and have no public utilities. Rio alone has 600,000 *favelados*. Their homes often have dirt floors and are sometimes swept down the hillsides during the rainy season. Alleys between houses are perhaps a few feet wide and are often filled with chickens, dogs, and sewage. For these new urbanites the future is bleak. Many work as domestics. Their children may fare better if they can stay healthy enough to survive childhood and receive enough education to learn a trade.

The catalog of emerging urban ills in cities abroad is all too familiar to Americans: drugs, congested living, racial tensions, generation gaps, outmoded education, juvenile delinquency, poverty. Like love and marriage, urbanization's blessings and problems go together. To paraphrase Marshall McLuhan, the "global city" as well as the "global village" is almost upon us. For better and for worse, urban influences are showing up in every corner of the world.

Chapter 2

# THE CHURCH IN THE CITIES

Lloyd Swantz's office in Dar es Salaam, Tanzania, looks like that of any city planner. Huge aerial photos of the city hang in one corner. Maps and diagrams cling to the walls. Papers and books are stacked on the shelves. One chart asks, "Has your church an urban ministry plan?" Then it lists the statistics:

    1891 — 14,000 population — 2 churches.
    1945 — 39,000 population — 10 churches.
    1969 — 300,000 population — 60 churches.
    1989 — 1,000,000 population — ? churches.

The church is reacting to urban Dar es Salaam. In 1920 only 1.5 percent of the city's population was Christian. By 1957 that figure had jumped to 15 percent. Now it is 32 percent. (Of the 100,000 Christians, 15,000 are Lutheran.) In 20 years the Christian population may be 50 percent.

Lloyd Swantz is happy to talk about the statistics he has gathered as director of the Urban/Industrial Mission of the Christian Council of Tanzania. But he's alarmed at some implications of the city's rapid church growth. The sheer number of people that the church will have to cope with calls for some drastic rethinking, he says.

"At present we have 70 places of worship to serve approximately 100,000 Christians. If we are to serve 400,000 additional Christians in the next 20 years, we need to build 14 new churches every year for the next

20 years. Currently we are only building two or three new churches a year."

Not all the urgency lies in the future. "Already," says Swantz, "we estimate that only about one-half of the Christians in Dar es Salaam are registered with any church. Many have come into the city from rural areas without transferring their membership from their home congregations. On an average Sunday about only one-fourth of these registered Christians attend services. This means that for every Christian inside the church, three are outside.

"The 70 places of worship perhaps feel satisfied because their churches are full on Sunday. One new church (Kinondoni Lutheran) with a 300-seat nave found that it was too small eight months after it was built. The reality is that our churches are only able to seat about one-fourth of the Christian population, and only about that number actually attend. This means that the church is gradually losing touch with more than one-half of its membership."

Statistics are not the whole story. Sociology enters the picture. "The question has to be asked," says Swantz, "whether the African urban dweller is a tribesman or a townsman. A great many people in the city are first generation urbanites. They still live with a foot in their rural background and a foot in their urban home." This means that the church must consider two things in urban ministry in Dar es Salaam: (1) the city's physical growth that now stands at 335,000 and, (2) the sociological adjustments of the people. The office of Urban Industrial Mission attempts to respond to both.

The church has the responsibility to help improve the life of the city, continues Swantz. So he helps congregations understand that Dar es Salaam needs 6,000 new homes a year, streets designed for thousands of cars and trucks instead of a few cars and many bicycles, and new water and sewage systems.

To fit the church into the physical perspective of the city, Swantz's office aided the congregations in preparing a church directory. What was intended to be a few pages of paper turned out to be a 38-page document. The 14 denominations in the city learned that they had a 177 Sunday services, 72 church organizations, 11 church schools and nurseries, and a host of other ventures. There were 500 clergy, sisters, evangelists, catechists, and full-time lay workers.

Swantz urges that churches secure at least two acres of land when they are considering a building program. He is serious when he asks them to consider their future parking needs. Locations, he says, should avoid heavy traffic intersections because of noise.

In order to alleviate the current shortages in buildings, Swantz has proposed the "house church." Although new churches in Africa often strive to get "a building, a bell, and an organ" like their American counterparts, African urbanites still like to gather in casual settings. Swantz thinks a front porch or underneath a tree is an ideal spot for a 20-member house church that meets once a week with a lay leader.

The idea was tested in one housing area and 15 house churches were soon in operation. Weekly services opened with Bible reading, followed by discussion of a topic such as youth, social welfare, marriage, or evangelism. Some social action was usually planned, such as visiting the sick on a certain street or starting a Sunday school. On occasion the Lord's Supper was celebrated and children baptized.

Of course, not every attempt at urban ministry is successful, particularly among students. Wilfred Mlay, a graduate of the University of Tanzania in geography and literature, says that "where I come from religion is a natural part of life. But here, in the urban areas, everything is a hodgepodge. Family and traditional ties are broken, and other influences take over. The church suffers."

Mlay is chairman of the university's Student Christian Fellowship. He is disturbed that although 72 percent of the university's enrollment is Christian, less than one-third participate in the student fellowship.

*The City is the Frontier*

On the other side of the African continent, a different sort of urban ministry was a long time in coming. One of the most incredible stories in mission history is that Lutherans went into Liberia in 1860, entering through the port city of Monrovia and going up the St. Paul River to establish the first mission named Muhlenberg. Subsequent churches and schools were established at 25-mile intervals up the river, eventually reaching about 200 miles inland.

As a result of this procedure, missionaries jumped over the city of Monrovia for nearly 90 years before the first Lutheran congregation was established in the city. St. Peter's Lutheran Church in Monrovia traces its history from 1947, when the first services were held, through 1951, when the congregation was organized, to 1957 when their modern church building was completed.

The Monrovia situation is perhaps the darkest example of how American missionaries sought the exotic and the unusual — taking the light of the Gospel into the darkness of the bush — but only lately seeing the urban field as equally ready for harvest. What has now happened at St. Peter's Church is that because of migration to Monrovia, the church literally has too many members. Monrovia has 100,000 residents, and even without a special program of evangelism 120 persons were baptized and 36 more transferred into St. Peter's in the first few months of 1970. Present statistics show that the church has 1,400 members — and three Sunday services.

In order to handle the mushrooming population,

St. Peter's has developed a neighborhood ministry. Groups are set up throughout the city where there are concentrations of membership or potential membership. Religious instruction is given at these centers, along with literacy training, music education, and worship. These groups are also centers for house-to-house visitation.

Basically the groups are satellites of St. Peter's congregation, feeding the growth and worship of the main congregation. At the same time, the groups may become mission congregations of St. Peter's and, if they grow strong enough, separate, self-supporting congregations. This concept is particularly appropriate since Monrovia is a city that stretches for 15 miles along the Atlantic coast, but only one mile inland. The centers provide a means of contact with people who migrate into the city and make religious instruction available near their homes. The cost of getting to St. Peter's is a drawback (a 10-cent bus ride is expensive to a laborer who earns $30 a month), so the centers are economically appealing. Every member of St. Peter's is expected to be a part of a neighborhood center as well as attend the main services at the church on Sunday.

*One Church and 35,000 People*

Halfway around the world in Singapore, Pastor John Nelson stands in front of Queenstown Lutheran Church. The brick structure with its sharply sloping roof is encircled by 10-story high-rise apartments that house 100 families each. As Pastor Nelson surveys the 360-degree circle of apartments, he notes that 35,000 people can see the cross on the church's exterior from their apartment balconies. He also knows that Queenstown is one of 40 such high-rise housing estates in Singapore.

Along with a shopping center and a market, the church forms the physical core of the Queenstown community. The apartments make an outer ring. In such a setting, one does not ask what role a church should play. One only asks how it plays it.

Pastor Nelson, one of few Singaporeans to sport a crewcut, has been answering that question with an action-packed program since the Queenstown church was completed in 1965. The freestanding altar in the middle of the worship area and the street noise that disturbs the worshiper during the service are constant reminders that the church is a part of all that is around it.

"Sunday is actually our slack day," says Nelson in his sharp, staccato voice. On Sunday the church has "only" English and Chinese Sunday school and church, a coffee hour, pastor's class, and evening worship. From Monday through Friday, a play center for 170 neighborhood preschoolers is operated in morning and afternoon shifts. Scheduled at other times during the week are Bible study, youth fellowship, classes in sewing, cooking, art, and harmonica, adult recreation, a chess club, Boys Brigade (similar to Boy Scouts), a church softball team, biddy basketball and softball, and choir practice. A library and study area are open daily.

But activity alone does not attract people. Pastor Nelson and Chinese pastor Loke Hoy San estimate that they have visited 1,500 apartments in the 18 buildings that surround the church. "We go directly into the buildings," Nelson explains. "There is no doorman, no locks. Often we visit the homes of kids who come to the play center, and tell their mothers about our cooking and sewing classes. We also find other youngsters who can come to Sunday school."

"See the balcony on that apartment house?" asks Bill Bolm, a 29-year-old American who directs the play center. "Look how narrow it is. Now you see why the church has to provide something for these kids to do." Bolm, a former football quarterback and coach, says that "these kids can still play ball when I leave. But if they 'have the Word,' then I'm thrilled. I look to see who comes to play *and* who comes to Sunday school and church."

"The hardest people to reach," says Pastor Loke, "are those who have no religious background. They see no need for religion. Those who are superstitious, or who follow ancestor worship, are easier to approach because they have some type of belief."

Neither Loke, Nelson, nor Bolm minimize the difficulties of ministry to Queenstown's apartments. "We occasionally get a door slammed in our face," admits Nelson. Despite the day-in, day-out activity, growth of the congregation is slow. Membership totals 90, with the average age of members about 25. Some 90 percent of the members are Chinese.

*For the Slum Poor*

Far removed from Singapore, but caught in the midst of intense urban surroundings, is a modern red-brick series of buildings on a hill overlooking Caracas, Venezuela. These are the buildings of the "Movimiento de Educación Popular" (Movement for Popular Education), a one-half-million-dollar layout funded by the Lutheran World Federation. About 250 youngsters from age 7 to mid-teens go there to learn reading and writing, carpentry, metal work, mechanical drawing, sewing, and nutrition. The basic intention is to teach youngsters a trade so they can boost themselves out of their slum homes that surround the school.

Hansruedi Peplinski, a 34-year-old Swiss-born pastor and educator, is principal of the school. After pointing toward Caracas which lay before us in the valley, he gave me a tour of the three school buildings, the grass campus, and the gravel driveway built on level land that had been gouged out of a mountain. The buildings stand in sharp contrast with the nearby houses built of hollow, reddish tile along the narrow streets.

Inside the school, display cases exhibited the woodwork and sewing of some classes. A skylight and a small indoor garden caught my eye. So did the terazzo floor. "We put the best in the buildings," Peplinski explains, "so the kids would learn what the best is and strive for it."

Sewing machines stood in neat rows in a room of the next building, while stoves, refrigerators, cabinets, and tables lined the walls of another room. In the woodworking shop, students have individual benches complete with a tool rack and storage area for wood. On the wall are examples of small trucks and animal pull-toys used to teach woodworking techniques.

After a student completes a project, he grades himself: B means *bueno* (good), A, acceptable, and D, deficient. Then he discusses his grade with the workshop master. "We do this to help the student learn to judge his own work," explained Peplinski. "Most of these youngsters have always been 'told' things by other people. We want them to think for themselves."

When I remarked about the size of such an undertaking, Peplinski replied, "Some people call me a dreamer, but I'm not. I'm very practical. The point is that other agencies are not involved in community work here, so the church must be."

"You can look at these *barrios* and get the wrong idea. A slum in the U. S. is something on the way down. In Caracas it's an area on the way up. The *barrios* are the least painful way of adapting these rural folk to 20th-century Venezuelan life.

"People who have fled the plantations in the interior find these conditions better than they had. After 10 or 12 years of this type of life, they're better adapted to make the transition to apartments and running water.

"The school is important because it prepares youngsters to be ready for the next transition. We try to change the kids from a rural to an urban mentality. In grades one through three, we teach reading, writing, and math.

In grades four through six, the basic courses are continued, but students also take courses in each of the trades. In the last 2 years, they concentrate on the trade that most appeals to them. When they finish, they'll have a basic understanding of all phases of a trade, not 'piecework' assembly-line training. We also encourage our students to become shop owners and be self-employed instead of becoming dependent on foreign-dominated businesses."

Peplinski's theories apparently work. "Movimiento de Educación Popular" has first graders as old as 10 and more applications than they can handle. Students pay $2 a month tuition if they can afford it. The only entrance requirement is that a child live in an urban slum of Caracas and be poor.

## Industrial Missions Too

Whether the church is ministering through urban strategy in Tanzania, high-rise apartment outreach in Singapore, or a school for slum poor in Venezuela, the message is the same: the church is going into the urban areas of every continent. The old stereotypes of missions overseas — the thatched huts, jungle paths, and uncivilized conditions — are out of date. And the main force that is moving the church to a cutting edge in world society is not simply a recognition of the world, but a new recognition of the church's role *in* that world. One cannot overestimate the extent to which urban ministry is possible virtually everywhere on the globe.

Curiously enough, a pattern of urban ministry which has been only moderately successful in America is faring much better overseas — industrial missions. Even a country with a large rural population such as India is trying them. A new community service center has been established in Madras, as well as a program for the development of social workers.

In Dar es Salaam, Tanzania, the church uses industrial contacts to reach young people who immigrate into the city's labor force. "In America and Europe, chaplains go into industries and talk to workers," says Lloyd Swantz. "But that approach doesn't work here. We don't have the money or the lunch bucket/thermos routine. We're more concerned that the working man's difficulties be kept constantly before the church. Last year we conducted five forums about the unemployed, the school-leaver, and the working woman. With trade unions concerned about the payment of the factory workers, the church is championing the cause of the domestic employee, the unemployed, and the unemployable."

In Petaling Jaya, a suburb of the Malaysian capital city of Kuala Lumpur, COM SUIM (Committee for Selangor Urban Industrial Mission) is a group of Roman Catholics, Anglicans, Methodists, and Lutherans who focus on the 250 factories and 10,000 employees that have come into the Petaling Jaya area in recent years.

"One problem," says missionary Dave Eichner, "is that authorities never seem to realize that factory workers get low wages and therefore need low-cost housing. Little cheap housing has been provided, so the need gets worse."

In dealing with another concern, COM SUIM staffer Shanta Moses organized women to protest the lack of flood controls in one part of Petaling Jaya. The women marched on the town board office and in spite of the negative attitude of officials, got their message across. Another project concerned a heavy accident rate on a particular highway. In one day 29 accidents had occurred along one stretch of the road. Leaflets were distributed describing the need for improvements in the road. Prayers were offered in churches; newspapers ran stories. Authorities decided to install two traffic lights, but the work was delayed so long that a second public effort was needed to get their installation.

Industrial missions are also sprouting in Sao Paulo,

Brazil. In the satellite city of Santo Andre, the Center for the Training and Education of the Family is open 3 days a week and serves 120 persons a month. Most of the counseling deals with family problems: child rearing, planned parenthood, and divorce.

"Industry didn't invite us in," says Brazilian pastor Karl Busch. "They didn't care about their employees' religion. We put up a notice in the town hall and other public places, and people began to come."

In Japan industrial missions take a slightly different turn. K. Yamamoto, a 45-year-old executive in the Toyo Kogyo automobile firm in Hiroshima, feels that "our number one management problem is the human factor. Before the war we could take loyalty to the company for granted. Now with life employment and excellent fringe benefits assured, our employees are still loyal, but they are asking questions. It's not just money they want; they want to know what they're working and living for. They come to us and say 'help us set up targets for ourselves.' So we try to find out through group discussion what moves them."

In another part of Japan, Pastor Masahara Oka in Nagasaki uses politics to effect change. On Saturday he is likely to be distributing tracts in front of a local high school. On Sunday he may preach on the newness of the Gospel. On Monday he may address a crowd at city hall. He is called the "peace pastor" by local newspapers and was elected to the Nagasaki city council on an independent ticket supported largely by Christians, A-bomb victims, Korean expatriates, and New Left students and laborers.

Mosquito control is a major concern of an industrial mission project sponsored by the Lutheran Church in Singapore. Focusing on Jurong Industrial Estate, an area of 20,000 residents that is expected to increase to one-half million in the next decade, the mission involves broad ecumenical cooperation on a variety of efforts—

from English language instruction to insect control.

*An Unexpected Problem — at Home*

Surprisingly enough, one problem related to urban ministry abroad concerns the church at home. Such overseas missions do not create the sense of the exotic which has traditionally had so much appeal for American churchgoers. Stateside people, particularly those caught up in the mechanical, technical, space-age rush and confusion, have seen in the old images of overseas missions a part of the past which they recall with nostalgia. The shift from the rural, and even primitive, lifestyles into more urban settings signals more than a shift within those countries. These new settings force Americans to alter their images in order to perceive the new realities of the overseas scene.

Churchgoers hesitate to do this. They see so much in their own backyards about the urban crisis — the difficulties between races and cultures, rebelling youth, the crime rate, congested streets — which they do not like, and which they would like to spare the rest of the world. Americans know all too well the transitions and problems the urban scene can bring.

So instead of giving greater support to overseas missions where the problems and joys of life are so similar to their at-home situations, the tendency is for church people to be less interested. The reason is that the thrill of the bush pictures and exotic ways are gone. Anyone who has ever addressed a study group knows that interest rises when you show a color slide of a grass hut; city scenes are ho-hum.

That's unfortunate for our friends abroad . . . but probably more devastating in the long run for us. Blinders will do Americans no good. The past cannot be reclaimed at home or abroad. The urban setting is a fact of life. And it is reaching into the uttermost parts of the church.

# Chapter 3

# CHURCH GROWTH YOU OVERLOOKED

Close your eyes, and imagine that you are attending the following worship services . . .

The road to Namo Ukur is narrow and bumpy. It starts out as paved, then becomes dirt. On either side is the tangled undergrowth so typical of northern Sumatra. Then a church with split bamboo walls and a palm thatched roof stands in a clearing amid a few houses and farm land.

"One thousand people will be baptized here next month," the heavily tanned chief of police of Namo Ukur tells me. He is a leader in the Karo Batak Church, but communications are so poor in much of Indonesia that he is probably not aware that his church is part of one of the most phenomenal mass movements in modern Christian history. Within the last half dozen years, more than 400,000 Indonesians have been baptized.

The congregation at Namo Ukur was founded only a couple of years ago with 300 members. Now that 1,000 more persons will be baptized, the simple church building will be far too small. So the baptism service will be held one quarter mile away at the village marketplace, a large cement area with a rusting tin roof. To one side is a spacious green clearing where worshipers will sit.

"We will begin with the regular baptism service," the chief of police continued (a man with the musical name of S. Sembiring). "Then the pastors—probably 25 of them—will come down to the edge of the open area, and people will line up in front of them. Each person will have his name written down and hand it to the pastor.

"Then we have speakers from the government, the military, and the church. It's an all-day affair, with music, a feast, and an auction to raise funds for the new church building we will need. Some people will come from as far away as eight or ten miles and will stay overnight."

The description staggers the imagination — 1,000 baptisms at one service! Such services are happening all over Indonesia. Reports circulate of 100,000 baptisms in the central Java Christian Church, and of a Roman Catholic mission that has 150 members and 2,000 persons receiving instruction. The Karo Batak Church of which the Namo Ukur Church is a part has grown 30,000 to 70,000 members in a few years. . . .

*A Sunday in Swahili*

The Sunday service is about to begin, but women in brightly colored dresses and headbands are still coming in, and little children with blue hymnals follow their mothers down the aisle. Their sandals make scratchy sounds on the concrete floor as the white-robed evangelist comes in and kneels before the altar. It's my first Sunday in Tanzania, and as far as I am concerned, it will be a Sunday in Swahili.

The congregation is located in Kinondoni, a section of the capital city of Dar es Salaam. As the evangelist begins the service, the words are strange, but it is easy to follow the outline of the service . . . invocation . . . confession . . . declaration of grace. Then the Introit is read, the evangelist intoning it in clear, strong Swahili. Africans like to sing and have fine rhythm. When they launch into the Gloria in Excelsis, it has a lot of glory in it. Similar sized American congregations would be put to shame.

There is a sermon. For 12 minutes the evangelist speaks about the Good Shepherd in a careful straightforward style. The subject is appropriate. Pastors in

Tanzania are called "Mchungaji," the Swahili word for shepherd. After the sermon, a commotion sets in that I do not understand. The choir is singing an anthem when suddenly people stand up and start walking toward the front of the church. Then I realize what is happening. Straw baskets have been placed on two chairs in the chancel area and people are going to the front, row by row, to give their offering. They are deliberate in their actions, carefully placing the money in the basket, palm down and kneeling slightly. Then they make their way back to their seat.

I expect the prayer to be next, but instead there's a short announcement, and the shuffling starts again. One person in the congregation wants to give thanks for recovering from an illness, and has asked his friends to join him in a special offering of thanksgiving. From all parts of the church, people get up and give a second offering.

The Kinondoni congregation is part of the remarkable church growth that is going on in Tanzania. In 1900, 3 percent of Africa's population was Christian. Today 28 percent is Christian. Within 30 years, Christians are expected to make up 46 percent of the population. . . .[1]

## A Congregation of 111,000

The young man standing on the platform was short and stocky, his hair wavy, and his eyes deep set. At one time he had been a house painter, but now he is a preacher. As he held his Bible open and jabbed the air with his finger, I could believe that 8,000 people would jam the church to hear him.

"Our services are more vivid than those of Billy Graham," Manoel de Melo was saying. "More like Oral Roberts. We heal, we get excited. When I preach, I wander around the aisles. The service may last two hours."

[1] David Barrett, "Church Growth Bulletin" (Palo Alto, Calif.), V, No. 5 (May 1969).

I looked up and down the long narrow hall. Natural finished wood met my eye everywhere — ceiling, walls, pews. The altar was a raised area at one side. But I could not find the organ.

"We don't use an organ," de Melo explained. "Organ music is monotonous, so we use band instruments to stir up excitement."

Outside this mammoth room, concrete walls outlined a new section that will increase the church's seating capacity to 25,000. A heliport and a social service center are also taking shape. Six-foot replicas of the Bible stand at the doorways, each emblazoned with a Scripture verse in Portuguese. Above, red and green neon lights illuminate the twilight: "Brasil Para Cristo" (Brazil for Christ).

This sprawling building rising out of the red clay of Sao Paulo, Brazil, is symbolic of the fastest growing religious movement in South America — the Pentecostal Church. The Sao Paulo congregation alone has 111,000 members. (That statistic is correct!) By contrast, Baptists in the city number 18,000; Presbyterians, 17,000. In the entire country the "Brazil for Christ" church has 1,100,000 members, 300 pastors, and 4,200 special workers and lay preachers. In 1968 "Brazil for Christ" became the largest Pentecostal church to join the World Council of Churches. One clergyman estimates that 50 percent of Protestant growth in South America today is Pentecostal. . . .

*Twenty-Five Remarkable Years*

From all parts of the world, the message is the same: church growth. The fruits of Western-initiated missions are incredibly impressive. Although American Christians tend to think of Asia as impenetrable, the continent has perhaps 80 million Christians. Seventy-five percent of the people in the Pacific islands are professing Christians. Outsiders don't realize that the city of Seoul, Korea, has 600 Christian churches. The church in Korea grew more from 1953 to 1960 than it had in the previous 60 years. Medical missionaries in Korea have produced 3,000 highly trained medical doctors. In Taiwan the Presbyterian Church had a "double the church campaign" between 1955 and 1965 and succeeded in its goal.

There are more church people of the Reformed and Presbyterian tradition in Indonesia today than in the United States. Some of the converts, probably 100,000, have come from the Muslim faith. But most have come from those who had previously followed tribal rites or spirit worship.

By the year 2,000 Christianity will likely be the major religion of Africa. An astonishing fact is that the center of Christianity, which in the early Christian era centered in the eastern end of the Mediterranean Sea, then moved into Western Europe and on to the United States in the 19th century—that center of Christianity may by the end of the century be lodged in Africa. This projection is even more phenomenal when it is realized that most of Africa's growth is occurring in the independent African churches, not in those related to Western denominations.

Indeed, Christianity is the major religion in sub-Sahara Africa. Over 1,100 people per day are added to church membership in Kenya—a figure which represents double the population growth in a nation that is 60 percent Christian. A new denomination comes into being every two weeks, and some 230 denominations are now registered in the country. In Zaire (formerly Congo), 83 percent of the population claims to be Catholic or Protestant.

In Latin America growth has taken different forms. Protestants in Brazil grew from 2 million in 1945 to nearly 20 million in 1970, partly through the Pentecostal fervor that is establishing new congregations at the rate of 3,000 a year. In the entire continent Pentecostals outnumber all other Protestant bodies two to one. In the area of mission schools, the largest engineering school in Latin America is church-sponsored.

Part of the difficulty in realizing this church growth around the world comes from the blinders which North Americans usually wear. Americans generally are short-sighted, not seeing what happens beyond their continental borders. They tend to be convinced that if the church is not doing well in the United States — or in the United States and Western Europe — then the church is not doing well anywhere in the world. Such a presumptive attitude is also a spillover of the general tendency of Americans to think about everything in their country in superlative terms.

Just the opposite of this narrow view is true. The church is actually growing dramatically everywhere in the world *except* in Western Europe, Scandinavia, and the United States. The Third World is not likely to remain third in the number of Christians. The astonishing fact is that Christianity as a world movement has hardly ever been in better shape. The last 25 years have been some of the most remarkable in all of Christian history. These 25 years are those between the horrible mushroom cloud over Hiroshima on August 14, 1945 and (lacking 21 days) man's first step on the moon in 1969.[2]

Such statements are not based on wishful thinking. The assumption that the Christian proportion of the population will decline as world population increases is not necessarily true. The biological growth of Christianity is not the only growth, because the church grows not only via births to Christians but also through conversions. In 1964 statistics showed that Protestantism had increased 18-fold in the previous 60 years in the non-Western world while the population increase was only two-fold. In virtually every place the Christian com-

---

[2] For an extensive and enlightening discussion of this phenomena, see Ralph D. Winter, *The Twenty-Five Unbelievable Years 1945 – 1969* (South Pasadena, Calif.: William Carey Library, 1970).

munity is growing as rapidly or more rapidly than the population — not in absolute numbers, but in growth rate and therefore in percentage of the population. In Brazil in 1970, for example, Protestants had an annual growth of 11.3 percent which means doubling in seven years, while the population of the country will take 24 years to double.[3]

*Three Closer Looks*

Several other things should be said about the phenomenal growth of the church in Indonesia, Africa, and South America. In Indonesia the growth has occurred largely in rural areas. Namo Ukur, mentioned at the beginning of this chapter, is a tiny village near the city of Medan in northern Sumatra, the largest of 3,000 islands that make up the nation of Indonesia. The islands parallel the Malay peninsula, curve under the equator and the Philippines, and eventually adjoin New Guinea. Indonesia is about twice the size of Texas, but if overlaid on a map of the United States, it would stretch from San Francisco to Bermuda. Its 112 million inhabitants are 85 percent Muslim and 7 percent Christian, with the rest Hindu, Buddhist, or animist.

One of the first questions that the new Christians ask in Indonesia is "what shall I do with my old religion?" One village elder tells converts that they should not condemn their former way of worship but leave it gradually. He told me about one community where residents thought the spirit of their ancestors lived in a banana tree. Consequently, a festival was arranged as a farewell to the old religion, a kind of saying "excuse us" to the religion of their ancestors. After that, said the elder, they were baptized.

A general secretary of the regional council of churches of Sumatra notes that "if one Batak leader is baptized,

<hr />

[3] R. Pierce Beaver, *From Missions to Mission* (New York: Association Press Reflection Book, 1964).

others will follow. Baptize 50 people in one place and the total will multiply by five in one year because of family loyalties." Another favorite saying is that "where you find one Batak, you will have a witness to his faith. Where there are two, you will have a prayer meeting. With four, you will have a choir. With ten, a congregation."

The rapid growth of the church in Africa is taking place in both the rural and the urban areas. In some rural areas of Ethiopia, growth comes rapidly because entire tribes or groups of people are converted. In more urban areas, such as Dar es Salaam in Tanzania, growth comes partly because of the influx of people from the country to the city. In that situation the church is one of the few parts of their former culture which they find in the city.

Lloyd Swantz, the urban church planner in Dar es Salaam, points out that the church has always been a pioneering force in Tanzanian life. He recalls that until 10 years ago 70 percent of the schools in the country were operated by the churches. So were most of the clinics and hospitals. Now, he says, the church is again on the growing edge because it is helping develop urban life. The city is now the frontier for the church, and converts are being won there just as they are on the rural frontier.

Swantz also notes at least two other reasons for growth. The first is births. A few years ago, the birthrate in Africa was 46 per thousand; the world average was 34 per thousand. The second reason is more profound, and gets to the heart of the mission enterprise. A belief in God is acceptable in Africa, Swantz says. The message of love and forgiveness releases people from the tensions of witchcraft and sorcery. Sophistication and affluence do not detract from the message as they often do in more developed countries.

The Pentecostal movement in South America is attracting many of the poor in both the urban and the rural areas. In Brazil the Pentecostals have 4 million adherents, twice as many as all other Protestant groups combined. In Chile they claim a million, probably one-tenth of the population.

North American mainline Protestants tend to dismiss Pentecostalism as simplistic and emotional. The Bible is interpreted literally, and worship includes more exuberance than Lutherans, Presbyterians, and Episcopalians think proper. But the reality is that North American mainline Protestantism is ailing in South America, and even the Roman Catholic Church is less than healthy. At the same time, the Pentecostals are lively and vigorous.

The point of these paragraphs is that startling church growth is taking place in various segments of society abroad, both rural and urban. Admittedly, none of the examples come from teeming metropolitan areas such as Tokyo or Singapore. But the lack of growth in such areas is probably not related to their urbanism. Rather, Christianity has traditionally had a difficult time in reaping large numbers of converts in areas that are predominately Buddhist or Confucian. Even when the missions in mainland China were at their height, the number of converts to Christianity was small in proportion to the population of the country. A Lutheran congregation in Nagaski, which was organized 14 years ago, has only 44 members today. The average Lutheran congregation in Japan is only about twice that size – small according to American standards. In Japan though, where Christians are a minority, church members tend to be more active.

*Expecting Great Things from God*

Regardless, these statistics from Indonesia, Africa, and South America, along with phrases like "the most remarkable 25 years in Christian history," thrill the hearts of churchgoers everywhere. The information is almost too good to believe. But more than that, they give substance and meaning to some of the Scripture passages familiar to us. "The Lord is the everlasting God, the creator of the ends of the earth," Isaiah wrote. "He does not faint or grow weary, His understanding is unsearchable. . . . Even youths shall faint and be weary, and young men shall fall exhausted; but they who wait for the Lord shall renew their strength; they shall mount up with wings like eagles; they shall run and not be weary; they shall walk and not faint." (Isaiah 40:28b-31 RSV)

These words no longer seem hollow when today's church growth is recalled. The soaring phrases of Saint Paul about giving thanks "unto Him who is able to subdue all things," and "the breadth and length and height and depth . . . of the wisdom and knowledge of God" take on new truth. We realize that the words of Scripture do not lie or speak naively. They speak the truth to those who expect to hear it.

Significantly, these things were all summed up by an English missionary, William Carey, in 1792: "Expect great things *from* God," he wrote, "and attempt great things *for* God." This type of attitude reflects more on us than on God. If we conceive of God as great, we will want to do great things for Him. If we are unimpressed with His potential, we will be haphazard in our response.

Great things *are* happening in the church abroad. The problem in the United States and Canada is that we haven't expected it.

# PHOTO ALBUM

After he was baptized, Langai Shing'adeda, former medicine man of Barabaig tribe in central Tanzania, took the name Musa (Moses), "one who leads his people out of darkness."

Lutheran missionary Daniel Nelsson (left) talks about industrial missions in Singapore with Harry Robinson, a Methodist who is mechanical manager of Mobil Refinery at Jurong Industrial Estate. Workers are at right.

Campus architecture is striking at University College, Dar es Salaam, Tanzania.

Police chief S. Sembiring (left) heads the lay evangelism program at Batak church in Namo Ukur on island of Sumatra in Indonesia. Nampat Surbakti (right) is a preacher and teacher.

James Allison (right), an ordained Lutheran deacon in Monrovia, Liberia, teaches story of the Ascension to Tuesday night neighborhood group.

45

Skyline of Dar es Salaam, Tanzania, shows Luther House (two rectangular buildings separated by round meeting hall) in heart of downtown.

Lutherans and Methodists operate this bookstore in downtown Monrovia, Liberia.

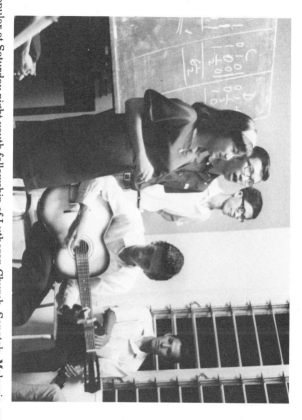

Guitars are popular at Saturday night youth fellowship of Lutheran Church, Sepatak, Malaysia, near capital city of Kuala Lumpur.

47

Pentecostal worshipers in Chile raise their hands and shout "Glory to God."

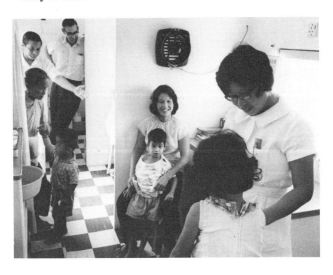

Nurse in mobile medical van treats patients in Malaysian village.

Vocational training school funded by Lutheran World Federation clings to mountainside in Caracas, Venezuela.

Principal George Anderson surveys new junior high school in Kota Kinabalu, Sabah (formerly North Borneo).

A new Christian in the village of Nagaredjo on the island of Sumatra, Indonesia.

Nearly 1,000 persons were baptized at this marketplace in all-day service in Namo Ukur, Indonesia. Local church was too small for the service.

This young man lives in church-operated Mtoni Boys Home in Dar es Salaam, Tanzania.

Azania Front Lutheran Church towers over downtown Dar es
Salaam, Tanzania.

Woman "feels the Spirit" in Pentecostal Church, Santiago, Chile.

Artwork has prominent place over altar in Pentecostal Church, Santiago, Chile.

# Chapter 4

# LAYMEN MAKE
# THE BEST EVANGELISTS

Their names are hard to pronounce. But Severo Wosoro, Shugate Dada, and Abagoli Wosoro, are evangelists in Ethiopia. When the Sudan Interior Mission entered southern Ethiopia in the early 1930s, it made contact with these three members of the Kembatta tribe. But before the missionaries could develop contacts with large groups of people, the Italians invaded Ethiopia, and the missionaries were forced to flee the country.

Since the three men were literates, they started a school and taught people to read the Bible. Before long, Abagoli became such a zealous evangelist that he was travelling the length and breadth of Kembattaland preaching and converting people. At times he was arrested and jailed by the Italians and later by the Ethiopian government. After questioning, they let him go, deciding that such a barely literate fellow was too ignorant to cause any trouble.

Abagoli didn't cause trouble. But when the missionaries of the Sudan Interior Mission returned to Ethiopia after World War II, they discovered 50,000 converts who could be traced to the work of the three men. The Kembatta synod is now a part of the Mekane Yesus Church, one of four Lutheran bodies in Ethiopia which comprise 91 percent of the nation's 153,000 Lutherans.

The lesson to be learned — and it may come as a shock to some of America's ordained clergy — is that laymen in Africa, Indonesia, Peru, New Guinea, India, and a number of other countries are largely responsible for the church's rapid growth in their areas. "I can't think of a single congregation in the last 2 years that was organized by an ordained pastor," a Methodist missionary told me on the Indonesian island of Sumatra.

In Ethiopia laymen are spreading the Gospel in the tribal territories in the Sidamo region without a central strategy or planned evangelism campaigns. When a Christian goes on a business trip or to visit relatives, he tells the Gospel message to any who haven't heard it. These occasional lay ministers number in the hundreds. Some, realizing that they have a special gift, begin making trips expressly for contacting non-Christian communities. They receive no pay.

In some Ethiopian communities where a layman has gathered a community of believers, the new group of converts sends a young man to the nearest Bible school for training. Upon completion he becomes their preacher. Even though this plan works well, the few pastors in the area remain hard pressed. One pastor, for instance, is in charge of three divisions in a single district. One division has 20 congregations, another 28, a third 14. Only the pastor can administer the sacraments to these congregations. But he supervises the work of 24 evangelists who lighten his load.

*The Preaching Policeman*

Indonesians learned the lesson of lay evangelists long ago. The Japanese invasion during World War II cut off the church from outside help and forced Dutch missionaries to leave. The Japanese closed schools, discouraged religious organizations, bled the land for their own purposes, and reduced the people to a near-starvation level.

But what seemed like a disaster ultimately laid the groundwork for the country's recent dramatic church growth. Laymen came to the rescue. In some areas church people returned to the leadership technique used in northern Sumatra by Ludwig I. Nommensen who brought Christianity to the area in 1862. Sent out by the Rhennish Mission Society of Germany, Nommensen enlisted the help of village chiefs in enhancing the people's receptivity to the Gospel. The police chief of Namo Ukur, S. Sembiring, is a modern-day Nommensen-helper.

Sembiring, a member of the Karo Batak Church (Lutheran), began contacting villages near Namo Ukur, asking for permission to conduct evangelistic services. Before long he found himself walking 14 miles several nights a week to conduct a service that began at 10 p. m. Often he does not get home until 3 a. m. Village chiefs welcome Sembiring and ask their people to listen. Sembiring prays, preaches, leads singing, and answers questions.

"Sometimes I spend so much time with the church that I get behind in my police work," he says. "But then, the crime rate has been going down since people became Christian. There's less stealing and gambling."

The only problem is that the Karo Batak Church has 200 congregations and only 20 ordained leaders. One of these pastors, P. Bukit, serves 20 parishes, including the Namo Ukur congregation. Each week Pastor Bukit gathers the elders from his 20 parishes and helps them prepare a sermon which they deliver in their congregations the following Sunday.

In the rural areas most of the elders are farmers, with a scattering of teachers and government workers. But if the elders come from the Djakarta area, they may include high-ranking military officers, businessmen, and jurists. Regardless of their background, they ask pointed questions about the Sunday texts. "What does it mean when God 'glorifies' Israel?" one wanted to know. "Spell out what is involved in the glorification." The pastor and his men probed the complex passage from Isaiah to determine its meaning in terms of their own situations.

After an hour they decided on a theme for the sermon and developed three points for an outline.

As might be suspected, some elders do an excellent job on Sunday; others do less well. The point is that despite a severe shortage of clergy, every pulpit in Indonesia is filled every Sunday.

Some areas have joint evangelism committees composed almost exclusively of elders. A group of 20 men from Batak, Javanese, and Chinese churches have gathered to train leaders in northern Sumatra to go back to their villages and teach people. Sri Hardono, a physician, personally organized a congregation in a village of 1,250 that now has 225 baptized Christians.

The laymen do more than evangelize and preach. They also teach instruction classes to new converts. "All people who volunteer to give Christian instruction are approved to do so," says one pastor. "Even though the church is growing so rapidly that we don't have enough teachers to go around, we want our new members to have 60 hours of instruction. We don't always manage to give them that much, but we get as close to it as possible."

The story of lay workers is nearly the same in India. Missionary Sam Schmitthenner, now president of Andhra Evangelical Lutheran Church, was at one time in charge of the licensed catechists and evangelists in the West Godavari Synod. "There was a shortage of pastors," said Schmitthenner. "One pastor may have to care for 15 or 20 churches. This meant that he would visit some of them only a few times a year."

The work of ministering to the people and their needs is carried on mainly by the licensed catechists and the Bible women. They live and work close to the people and are responsible for most of the conversions. During the time when Schmitthenner was in charge of the catechists and evangelists, some catechists were ordained as assistant pastors so that the sacraments could be given between the visits from the pastor.

*The Nurse Is a Tentmaker*

A similar concept is under way in Liberia. The people at St. Peter's Church in Monrovia have incorporated "tentmaking" into their ministry. Joseph Allison, a second grade teacher, and James Wolobah, a surgical nurse, have become ordained deacons of the church. They have pastoral authority to baptize and give the sacraments —but only at St. Peter's Church, not for the whole Lutheran Church in Liberia. The pastor of St. Peter's taught Allison and Wolobah a course in basic Christian doctrine.

Each man continues his regular job and serves the church part time. "It isn't hard to hold down two jobs," says Wolobah. "I only work at the eye hospital in the mornings. It doesn't affect my time at the church."

Allison, a pleasant, soft-spoken father of four, is described by St. Peter's pastor as a "born teacher." He came to Monrovia in 1960 to attend the University of Liberia, taught in St. Peter's School (kindergarten to grade 6) and assisted with pastoral duties from 1961 to 1964. Then he studied for 2 years at Augustana College in Sioux Falls, South Dakota. Upon his return to Saint Peter's, he began assisting on Sundays at the Kpelle service and conducting baptism instruction in Kpelle.

Both men are in charge of neighborhood centers in various parts of Monrovia. Their ministry involves visiting and teaching in the centers, as well as assisting at St. Peter's Sunday services. On a Tuesday night shortly after 7 p. m., I dropped by the neighborhood center in a section of Monrovia called Sayetown. The community borders on a paved road that leads past the magnificent Executive Mansion and government buildings in Monrovia. But Sayetown does not share that splendor. Its streets are sandy paths more suited for walking than for cars. Homes and stores are arranged haphazardly, a mixture of shacks and cement walls. At night kerosene lamps flicker, and small faces peer out of doorways.

In a tin-roofed, open-air building, I spotted Allison, who had gathered 17 adults and a host of children around him. He had placed several pictures on a chair and was telling the story of the Ascension. His words flowed in smooth, easy Kpelle, and the people listened closely. Passersby stopped to look. A single light bulb, suspended on a cord from the rafters, swung gently behind Allison.

The tentmaking concept being used so successfully by Wolobah and Allison is not new to Liberia. The country's late president, William Tubman, was a lay Methodist preacher. The new president, William Talbert, has been president of the World Baptist Alliance.

Tentmaking ministry began in the Lutheran Church in Peru in 1969. The first "lay pastor" was commissioned to return to his home near Cuzco. The result has been two additional congregations in the area, one Spanish speaking, and the other using the Quechua Indian language. Plans are under way to open a "roving theological school" for training tentmakers in the Peruvian ministry.

In Taiwan lay ministry takes a different twist. The church has grown rapidly, but as the country has urbanized, many of the present pastors are not as educated as many of the laymen. A distinct future role for the laity in Taiwan lies in training them to reach this more educated strata of society that is now sealed off from pastors because of social and cultural reasons. Some observers say that the laity are the key to church renewal in Taiwan.

The experience of the Evangelical Lutheran Church in New Guinea brings us full circle to the experience of the three men and the 50,000 converts in Ethiopia. The New Guinea church has 370,000 members, an increase of nearly 600 percent since World War II. At that time, missionaries were forced to leave, and much of the mission and church property was destroyed during the fighting. But Christians rebuilt their churches and schools, and enlisted lay workers now number 1,885. By contrast, there are only 236 pastors. The lay workers are largely self-supporting, earning their living within the usual village economy of New Guinea.

In part this pattern is built on the tradition established in 1908 by German missionary Christian Keysser, who called upon able-bodied men and women in his congregation to "dwell among the inland tribes, befriend them and win them by an exemplary Christian life." Since that time, thousands of Christians have become evangelists, adding village after village to the church.

*You Are a Minister*

The example of lay ministries, as performed throughout most of the Third World, is an obvious lesson for the American church. Curiously enough, the lesson should be traveling in reverse. The doctrine of the priesthood of all believers is common to virtually every American church that has sent out missionaries. But somehow, the new Christians abroad have grasped the potential strength of the doctrine with greater fervor and imagination than their parent churches.

Despite pronouncements from the pulpits, position statements by church conventions, and even the inner knowledge of individuals that they *are* the church, the task of the church in North America remains largely in the hands of the ordained clergy. Unfortunately, perhaps, for the sake of developing a lay ministry, North American churches have not been faced with the onslaughts of war, foreign occupation, and dwindling manpower which brought about the development of lay ministries in various parts of the world. These ministries, in addition to being a fulfillment of a central point of Christian faith, bring with them an authenticity of witness which is impossible to overestimate.

To their credit, some American mission agencies have learned the lesson to the extent that the trend in missionary personnel today is shifting toward the layman rather than the ordained man, the short-term instead of the career term, and the technician rather than the preacher. Specialists are being sent. A radio man to Tanzania, for example, or a farm manager. Or a business manager to the church in Malaysia and Singapore. A pilot to Liberia. In some rather surprising ways, the ministry of the American layman is often more visible overseas than in the United States.

The life styles of today's missionaries have changed also. Missionaries are not "different" people anymore. They are not expected to be overly pious. Rather they are an up-beat group, continuing to be their lively, joyful, and energetic selves just as they would in America.

This change is especially noticeable among the young people who take advantage of short-term opportunities available through the "Prince of Peace Volunteers" of The Lutheran Church—Missouri Synod, and the "M-3" program of the Lutheran Church in America. In this later program, the capital letter refers to the country where the young person will serve three years. "M," for example, stands for Malaysia. "T" means Tanzania.

Jeff Littleton, an M-3, is 25. His home church is Our Redeemer in Wauwatosa, Wisconsin, a congregation of The Lutheran Church—Missouri Synod. He teaches English in Grik and Lenggong, Malaysia. "I wanted to get out and do something different," says Jeff. "For the past 8 years I worked part time in a clothing store but I've had a great desire to be in church work. My generation can have an exciting time working in the church."

Mariya Futchs is also 25. Her home church is Messiah, Denver. She teaches English in Ipoh, Malaysia. "People here are more willing to accept a Peace Corps worker than a missionary because they have heard the old line that we "give" to them because we want them to join a church. So we try to be a Christian subtly instead of obtrusively. Preaching, for example, is not our way of interpreting Christianity. We do it through action and example and working with the whole person. It's not enough to be concerned just with people's faith. We have to help improve their physical situation too."

The point remains. Laymen are making the difference in churches abroad.

Chapter 5

# WHEN CHRISTIANS
# DO THINGS TOGETHER

Three percent of the population in Malaysia and Singapore is Christian. About half of that three percent is Roman Catholic. Of the remaining one-half, only about 10,000 are Lutheran.

The meaning behind those statistics hit me hard. When Christians are only three percent of the population, they must work together if the church is to have any impact on local affairs. In fact Christians must work together if they are going to be visible at all. Simply being Christian is being distinctive in Malaysia and Singapore – not to mention being Methodist or Lutheran!

Christians in Malaysia and Singapore have realized this factor more quickly and with more tolerance than Americans who still think in terms of congregational graveyards and the four different congregations that occupy four corners of a local square. In Petaling Jaya, a suburb of Malaysia's capital city of Kuala Lumpur, three congregations – Good Shepherd Lutheran, St. Paul's Anglican, and Trinity Lutheran – have cooperated in study courses in Lent. During the Week of Prayer for Christian Unity, services were exchanged between Protestant and Roman Catholic churches, with a Salvation Army chaplain preaching at the concluding service in a Roman Catholic cathedral. During a Lutheran Bible study series, 10 of 46 participants were Roman Catholic.

Ministerial students – whether they be Anglican, Lutheran, Presbyterian or Methodist – are trained together at Trinity Theological College in Singapore.

64

"When you come here, you become newly aware of what it means to be Lutheran," said Danraj Victor of Kuala Lumpur. "But because we've been here, we'll be better able to work with other Christians later."

Danraj is one of seven Lutheran students attending Trinity College. The institution was founded in 1948 by the Methodist, Anglican, and Presbyterian churches. At that time its enrollment was seven students and three professors. Today the student body totals 56, the majority of whom are Methodist. Seventeen professors make up the faculty, most of them Presbyterian.

"You'd be surprised at how easily such cooperation works," says Dr. Nord Simonsson of the Church of Sweden and a specialist in communications. "We have different systems of thinking about the theology, but we find that at the bottom of the matter we are much the same. We act as men in society, and there is where each of us is Christian."

*Of Sunday School Books and Television*

The experience among congregations and theological education in Malaysia and Singapore is typical of that around the world. Let me broaden the scope with some staccato-like references:

*Brazil.* Cooperation in feeding and clothing the poor and homeless has been an interdenominational effort for many years. In Brazil Lutheran World Relief and Church World Service combine to distribute food through 1,500 Protestant, Jewish, and civic agencies throughout the the country. In a recent year 270,543 persons in Brazil received 25,972,527 pounds of milk, wheat, corn meal, flour, vegetable oil, and other food. In India Lutheran World Relief distributed 2,000 tons of food, 90,000 blankets, and clothing and soap in 1971.

*Tanzania.* Like most countries that are approaching urbanization, Tanzania has an ecumenical agency titled the Christian Council of Tanzania. One project related to it is urban missions — with Lutheran and Anglican staff workers and a governing board headed by a Roman Catholic.

The council has also sponsored an ecumenical Christmas pageant in the national stadium in Dar es Salaam, and a joint Easter procession that gathers participants from each church enroute to a city park. The annual Reformation service is held in a Roman Catholic community center. Lutherans, Anglicans, and Moravians have developed a common liturgy and are working on a joint hymnal.

*Sabah.* The Basel Christian Church in Sabah ministers primarily to the Chinese in this part of Malaysia that was formerly known as North Borneo. But 19 years ago a Swiss mission society began ministering to the Kadazans, a tribal people who speak their own dialect. The Kadazans are a primitive people, generally living in longhouses. Each family has a room along one side of the house with everyone sharing a porch on the other side. They are friendly people, and when they smile, the men reveal lips stained red from the betel nuts they chew. The women often have a wad of tobacco wrapped around one of their front teeth.

The mission to the Kadazans has developed into the 6,000-member Protestant Church of Sabah; the older, Chinese-related Basel Christian Church and the newer, Kadazan-related Protestant Church of Sabah are working toward merger.

In Kota Kinabalu, capital of the state of Sabah, the student body president of the Basel Christian Church's junior high school is Wong Fook Kui, a Buddhist. At a similar church school in Sandakan, the president is Peter Cheng, a Roman Catholic. His assistant is Mohammed Zain, a Muslim. Both schools are partially supported by the Lutheran Church in America.

*Argentina.* Lutheran seminarians study at Union Seminary in downtown Buenos Aires in classes made up of Methodists, Anglicans, Waldensians, Presbyterians, and Disciples of Christ. The relatively small Lutheran community in Argentina has always been handicapped by the great diversity of national and cultural backgrounds of its members. As many as a dozen different countries, languages, and church traditions have been represented. But gradually they are approaching the ideal of a cohesive national Lutheran fellowship embracing them all.

*Liberia.* A joint Christian education curriculum has been designed by the Lutheran and Methodist churches. This Sunday school curriculum is written by Liberians for Liberians and is published jointly by the two denominations. A television project titled "Concern" is produced in Monrovia by these two churches. Lutherans and Methodists also jointly operate a bookstore and an audiovisual film library.

*India.* Andhra Christian Theological College trains pastors for the Andhra Baptist churches, the Church of South India, the South Andhra Lutheran Church, and the Andhra Evangelical Lutheran Church. The principal of the college is Dr. William D. Coleman, a missionary of the Lutheran Church in America.

*Trinidad.* It seems increasingly certain that the establishment of a Lutheran church is neither warranted nor intended in the face of the ecumenical reality of Trinidad. Since 1966 the Lutheran mission has been a member of the Christian Council of Trinidad and Tobago, which includes the Roman Catholic and Anglican churches. Lutherans are also observers in discussions going on intermittently between Presbyterians, Moravians, and Methodists. The purpose of the Lutheran involvement is to support existing congregational life in Trinidad by working through the Christian Council and specific denominations.

*Japan.* The seminary of the Japan Evangelical Lutheran Church and the United Church lie in the shadow of International Christian University, an interdenominationally supported school of high academic standing. Also recently established is an ecumenical institute, composed of individuals from the Roman Catholic, Orthodox, and various Protestant churches. The institute seeks to cooperate in practical projects of Christian witness; the first effort is the publication of a common Bible translation.

*Ethiopia.* The Radio Voice of the Gospel is beamed to target areas in Africa, Asia, the Near East, and the Far East over two 100-kilowatt shortwave transmitters located in Addis Ababa. Broadcasts go out in 17 languages, covering 30 countries and approximately one billion people. The station is owned and operated by the Lutheran World Federation broadcasting service and is affiliated in broadcasting with various Protestant groups.

*Hong Kong.* The Hong Kong Christian Council was established in 1954 and today represents about 75 percent of the Protestant church membership. Members of the Hong Kong clergy group also meet monthly and present papers on current theological and social issues. The first ecumenical worship by Protestants and Roman Catholics has taken place. The Lutheran Seminary has sponsored lectures by members of the Protestant and Catholic faith. The Lutheran household in Hong Kong remains partially divided. The Evangelical Lutheran Church of Hong Kong and The Lutheran Church — Missouri Synod mission do not have pulpit and altar fellowship — a reflection of the stateside situation.

*Ghana.* The Lutheran Church — Missouri Synod mission has a wider interest in Ghana than that of building up a sizable Lutheran church. Veteran missionary James Dretke is deeply involved in making a distinctive confessional contribution to the upbuilding of the entire Christian community in the country. This contribution is made in three major ways:

1. Dretke has been working with the ecumenically oriented "Islam in Africa" program. He visits Christian churches of all brands and teaches their leaders and members how to approach Muslims more effectively with God's Word; how to develop a sympathetic understanding of Muslim beliefs, biases, and taboos; and how to present the Gospel in a way that is winsome rather than repulsive.

2. Another LC-MS missionary and a Ghanian pastor work with the "Good News Institute" to deepen the Biblical and theological undergirding of leaders of the independent, indigenous, Pentecostal-type churches that are growing at such a rate that they will soon constitute a major sector of African Christianity. This effort is also an interdenominational venture.

3. In the industrial port city of Tema, Missouri leaders have joined with other Protestants and Catholics in an overall ecumenical strategy for developing parish ministries in all neighborhoods in accordance with a common pattern including community social services. One part of the strategy is an urban industrial ministry.

*Fiji.* After World War II, churches in the Pacific needed training for pastors — predominately Anglicans, Congregationalists, and Methodists, along with Lutherans in New Guinea. A seminary was established on the island of Fiji, and one of the professors is an American Lutheran Church clergyman under call from the Board of World Missions of the Lutheran Church in America.

*Singapore.* In designing Jurong Industrial Estate, a 17,000-acre high-rise apartment and manufacturing complex, the government of Singapore allotted one "religious" site for the building of a church. Lutherans, Roman Catholics, and Baptists bid for the location. When it was awarded to the Lutherans, the Lutheran Church in America and the Lutheran World Federation invested $165,000 to erect a church and a civic center. Jurong

Christian Church rises like a fortress on a corner opposite a shopping center on the estate.

The use of the word "Christian" in the church's name is deliberate. Since the church is the only one on the estate, candidates for baptism are instructed in the Lutheran faith, but members of other churches become "affiliate" members without officially changing their previous denominational alliances. The liturgy is largely Lutheran, although not identical to that in the *Service Book and Hymnal* of the Lutheran Church in America and the American Lutheran Church, or the *Lutheran Hymnal* of The Lutheran Church — Missouri Synod. Swedish Lutheran missionary Daniel Nelson, who heads the pastoral staff at Jurong, is assisted in visiting, leading worship, and industrial mission activity by an Anglican priest and a Methodist pastor. At present, more than 150 factories have been built at Jurong, employing 20,000 workers.

*Jamaica.* Sheldon Dewsbury, a 27-year-old Baptist from Trinidad, is a student at the United Theological College of the West Indies in Kingston, Jamaica. Sheldon is one of 80 students, of whom 19 are Methodist, 16 Baptist, 15 Moravian, 15 Anglican, 9 Presbyterian, 6 from the Lutheran Church in Guyana, and 2 from the United Church of Jamaica and Grand Cayman.

*Two Related Factors*

A number of the preceding illustrations refer to councils of churches. In all fairness it should be noted that Christian councils play a more important role in the underdeveloped countries abroad than they do in the United States. One reason is that Christian councils overseas can command resources which individual churches cannot. Individual churches can draw only upon the resources of their parent mission boards. But when the local churches, and through them their mission boards, cooperate, they can call on ecumenical agencies for assistance in the production of literature, radio and television work, refugee services, literacy services, and such joint efforts as industrial missions.

The councils also have more clout with the local government. When India cracked down a few years ago on the granting of visas to persons from non-Commonwealth countries, those churches which entrusted negotiations to the National Council of Churches of India fared better with the government than stateside mission boards that negotiated with the government alone. Governments can challenge and defeat churches one by one, but such action is much less likely when churches work together.

A second concern developing in mission circles is termed "multinational" or "multi-agency." Translated, these terms mean that it is no longer desirable for one Lutheran church in the United States to be the sole link to an overseas Lutheran church. Rather, it is better for autonomous churches overseas to have official relationships with several churches in America and Europe. The process reflects both the ecumenical nature of the church and good world strategy.

Since 1860, for example, the Lutheran Church in Liberia has been related only to the Lutheran Church in America. At present, efforts are under way to make the Liberian church related to more of the world Lutheran family. It is hoped that either Swedish or German mission societies will establish a relationship with the church.

In Tanzania 16 American and European mission agencies assist the program and personnel needs of the Evangelical Lutheran Church of Tanzania. The Taiwan Lutheran Church is related to two Norwegian mission societies, one Danish mission society, one Finnish mission society, the American Lutheran Church, and the Lutheran Church in America. The Lutheran Church of Chile and Peru are related to both the United Evangelical

Lutheran Church of Germany and the Lutheran Church in America.

The Northern Evangelical Lutheran Church in the Santal region of India has Norwegian, Danish, and United States mission boards. The Lutheran Church in New Guinea is related to the American Lutheran Church, the Lutheran Church in Australia, and a German mission society.

A number of factors make multinational and multiagency relationships desirable. One is that when a mission field is related to more than one parent church, the danger of cultural imperialism is considerably less. Missionaries have long been accused of instilling their culture in the people as well as their religion. When several outside agencies support a local church body, the cultural overlays are not nearly so predominant. Another factor encouraging these relationships is the flexibility and strength of support that can come from combined efforts. The approach is also evidence of the oneness of the church's mission.

When pushed to its logical conclusion, the concept of several agencies relating to autonomous churches results in the sharing of resources rather than the old practice of one supporting the other. Striking evidence of this development is that the Lutheran World Federation in 1970 changed the name of its "Department of World Mission" to "Department for Church Cooperation." The word "mission" was dropped because nearly all mission efforts today are cooperative ventures among autonomous churches.

Two years later, when the Lutheran Church in America was restructuring its boards and commissions, the division that was eventually named "World Mission and Ecumenism" was nearly termed simply "Interchurch Cooperation." The reason for retaining the phrase "world mission" was that too many churchgoers would wonder if the church were going out of the "mission" business. Not at all. The restructuring process was simply acknowledging that missions today are cooperative. The Lutheran Church in America, for example, is currently related to 16 churches in Africa, Asia, and Latin America. But all 16 churches are autonomous and by 1980 will be fully self-supporting, maintaining their own congregational and central administrative structures.

It may be that these examples of ecumenism overseas — from cooperative seminary training to joint Christian education curricula to councils of churches — provide a message to churches in the United States. To some it may seem ironic that the supporting churches — both among denominations as well as within the various Lutheran groups from the United States, Germany, and Scandinavia — should find cooperation more easily accomplished abroad than at home. Confessional commitment is a serious concern for Lutherans. Whether further consultation and dialogue will lead to a greater unanimity on the home front remains to be seen.

# Chapter 6

# SEE WHY THEY GROW

Everyone knows that a map of the world from 1945 is hopelessly out of date. In the years 1945 to 1970 the realignment of the world has approached the unbelievable. At least one historian has called it the "retreat of the West."

In 1945, 99.5 percent of the non-Western world was under Western domination. From 1946 to 1949, over 82 percent of the non-Western world that had been under the domination of the West received independence. These are the countries of Jordan, the Philippines, Pakistan, India, Japan, Burma, Ceylon, North Korea, Israel, South Korea, Laos, mainland China, Cambodia, and Indonesia.

From 1950 to 1955 Libya, North Vietnam, South Vietnam, and Egypt gained independence. From 1956 to 1960, 24 countries attained independence, most of them in Africa, such as Ghana, Togo, the Ivory Coast, but also others such as Malaysia and Cyprus. From 1961 to 1965 another 17 countries became independent. Ten more gained independence between 1966 and 1969. (The author is indebted for data to Ralph D. Winter, *The Twenty-Five Unbelievable Years 1945-1969.*)

The era of colonialism was over, for 99.5 percent of the non-Western world was independent by 1970. This is an exact reversal of the situation of 25 years previous. The implications of this emerging nationalism cannot be overemphasized in analyzing the current state of church missions. The development of indigenous leadership in the church is a natural expression of this nationalism, and a movement exceedingly healthy for both the church and the nation.

Only a handful of overseas ministers supported by one major denomination are continuing the traditional role of congregational pastor. In 1971 alone, nationals replaced missionaries in the following positions: high school principal in Malaysia, seminary professor in Tanzania, seminary president in Hong Kong, nursing instructor in Liberia, literature society director in Hong Kong, and high school teacher in Tanzania. Over 4,000 national workers serve in the 10 overseas churches related to this mission board.

Sensitivity to the presence of Westerners is rising in most countries also. Some restrict teachers and allow evangelistic missionaries (Japan). Others restrict evangelistic missionaries and allow teachers (India). Another country will allow neither (mainland China). Still another puts a 10-year limit upon a missionary's presence in the country (Malaysia). After that time he may be replaced, but no one person can spend a missionary career in the country. In addition to these restrictions, the presence of a Western missionary may be a negative factor for both the church and the country, whereas a generation ago the missionary had a national, cultural, and professional aura that was highly valued.

In the future the number of missionaries sent abroad — at least in the traditional definition of that term — will be fewer. One major denomination reduced its missionary force by 42 during 1971. In 1969 this denomination filled 265 missionary positions overseas. Today it has 198.

As world leaders in economy and commerce have learned, those who are self-supporting have self-respect. Moreover, those who have their own leaders make a more genuine and believable witness to their fellowmen. One of the new members of the Setapak congregation near Kuala Lumpur, Malaysia, is a young man named Stephen Kit Boom Kim. He selected the name Stephen when he was baptized because he had faced opposition from his parents and friends when he decided to join the church. But his actions started a chain reaction, and a number of other youths were baptized into the Setapak congregation. "These young people are good evangelists," says the pastor of the church. "They show the Setapak people a Christian who is an Oriental like themselves."

To help overseas churches become a significant factor in their emerging nations, American mission boards are asking what the church's role should be in such countries. Sometimes the answers are surprising. In Tanzania, for example, the church is lending its weight to a sociological concept called *ujamaa*, the Swahili term for "familyhood." A university chaplain describes it as "a tribal religious phenomenon that has been expanded into a political-economic-sociological base for forming a nation."

In simple terms, *ujamaa* is socialism. In a *ujamaa* village (where nomadic tribes are encouraged to settle for the sake of improving education, sanitation, medical facilities, and income), the people work together to produce a cash crop with profits being split among those who grew it. There is also opportunity for some land to be farmed privately. In some ways the village is comparable to an Israeli *kibbutz*. It is also reminiscent of the early days of Christianity, when Jesus' followers were communalistic, pooling their resources to maintain a common community. Politicians in America, though, consider this philosophy socialistic.

"As a church, Christians have the most to lose from socialism," says Herbert Haferman, president of the Lutheran Church of Tanzania's Eastern and Coastal Synod. "Most of our people are part of the elite here, and the churches are part of the establishment. Nevertheless, we have embraced the philosophy of the country because it is a good blending of theology and national purpose.

"There are critics, of course. Some say socialism doesn't take human nature or good theology seriously enough. People are not naturally altruistic, they say. Ultimately they will work for themselves and socialism will fail."

Perhaps. But at the moment, the overwhelming evidence in Tanzania is that *ujamaa* will succeed. With success, self-reliance will take over. And self-reliance will be the foundation for greater strength. Already financial, personnel, and scholarship aid to the Evangelical Lutheran Church in Tanzania is being reduced by some of the supporting churches. At the same time the church is growing. One estimate says there will be 351 million Christians in Africa by the year 2000. If so, a large reason is that people know that the church, like the country, is now free to a large degree from dependence on outside help. The church benefits from Third World nationalism.

*Of Politics and Sociology*

It is virtually impossible to separate politics from nationalism. In Indonesia politics has played a surprising role in the rapid growth of the church. In a nutshell, a great many conversions are the result of political expediency. "If you're Christian, you're not communist" is one way of saying it.

When President Sukarno took over the leadership of Indonesia after centuries of Dutch colonial rule, he denounced Westerners, pulled out of the United Nations and eventually turned "pink." The Indonesian Communist Party infiltrated nearly every village and became the third largest in the world. In September 1965 an attempted communist *coup* was repulsed by the Indonesian army, and a political blood bath followed with an estimated slaughter of a quarter million suspected communists.

During these years, Batak church leaders stood strongly against the communist influence even though acknowledging certain "suggested sermons" from the Ministry of Religion in Djakarta. Some church members even asked the church to support the communists. But during the retaliatory measures after the attempted coup, most Christians did not participate, or if they did, they turned over suspected communists to the army instead of killing them themselves.

These two factors made the Indonesian church stand out as a center of sanity amid chaos. "We did not condemn people as the Muslims did, but spoke of sin and grace, of love and forgiveness," says Karo Batak church president Angappen Ginting-Suka. "Church members who had been communists at the time of the attempted coup were excommunicated and then reinstated when they repudiated their communist leanings."

Then the Indonesian government interpreted the belief in God as stated in the *Five Principles* of the constitution to include only Christians, Muslims, and Hindus. Everyone was strongly advised to belong to one of those faiths. Tribal customs and animism were not recognized as official.

"Indonesians remembered that the church had not been so harsh with people after the coup and that Christianity had established many good schools and hospitals," says the president of the Karo Batak Church. Some villages adopted the faith en masse and erected a sign, "This is a Christian village." One group of villagers said they remembered a group of Christian youth who had camped overnight in their village. Over the years, they had not forgotten the behavior and spirit of "those young Christians." Another church official said that "people had expected Sukarno to lead them into the modern world, and when he failed them, they turned to religion to fill the void."

Sociological developments also affected the Indonesian church. In the mid-1960s many Indonesians began to migrate from the agricultural hinterlands to the costal urban areas, leaving behind not only their homeland, but their "home" religion.

"The tribal worship familiar to these kind of people depends on a closed community," explains United Methodist missionary Richard E. Brown. "It needs a separate, private kind of existence. But urbanization opens up a community. As a result, Christianity is identified with progress and modernity and offers the kind of security people have to leave behind when they forsake the villages. In order to reestablish their identity and community people turn to the church.

"These people who moved into the more urban areas and converted to Christianity from animism have done so with a great deal of conviction," continues Brown, "because their old religion was a way of life as well as a religion. The situation in Indonesia is not like the revivalistic, emotional experience of American history. The rapid conversions in Indonesia are a peculiarly Indonesian phenomenon, the result of some political unsettlings, some sociological upheavals, and the incredible amount of lay ministry by members of the Batak church."

Pastor Charles Koons makes similar statements regarding the growth of the church in Monrovia, the capital of Liberia. "In the villages where many people used to live, life is secure and closely knit. In the city this is gone. There's no close authority for them to turn to. The church attracts people from the rural areas because they find something of their past ties when they attend the church."

*People Movements*

As important as one-to-one communication of the Gospel may be, "people movements" bring larger numbers into the church. The phenomenon of 1,000 baptisms at a single service in Indonesia is one aspect of such a movement. Other striking examples come from Liberia and Ethiopia.

A "people movement" takes place when a group within a society starts to move into the church. The group is roughly similar in many ways. They may all live in close geographic proximity. They may speak one language. They may be descended from a common ancestor or group of ancestors. They may have been worshipping one basic superstition. They may suffer from the same problems: poverty, lack of water, or minimal education. They may earn their living in similar ways and have similar ethical or tribal codes.

All these factors make the participants conscious that they are a group. They know why they are different from other people who live in adjacent areas.

This group which sees itself as a unified whole instead of as individuals is also likely to receive the Christian message and become Christian as a group. Such a strategy is opposite that which is normally practiced in Western cultures. Almost invariably Americans think of religious conversion as something that happens to an individual.

But this is probably not the way in which our ancestors were first converted. They were likely approached as a total community by a single itinerant preacher. Nor is the individualistic approach the best way for churches to grow today in pagan populations. When attempts are made to build up the church in a non-Christian land by the baptisms of individuals, converts frequently find that they are ostracized by their friends, separated from their families, and cut off from the culture of their people. This kind of church is put together largely by loyalty to a missionary rather than by the church's adoption by the people as a part of their culture and an attempt to minister to their needs.

The "people movement" deals with this problem. By recognizing the principle that church growth comes in group fashion, whole communities are received into the fellowship of Christ with minimal disturbance to their culture. This approach not only preserves a way of life they have known, but also frees missionaries from the charge of "bringing their culture with their Bible."

To illustrate the people movement strategy: Liberian children used to be expected to attend mission school and then go back to their villages and evangelize their families. But instead of returning home, many students migrated to the larger cities in search of jobs or remained as assistants to the missionaries. Thus the Christian message seldom confronted the culture of Liberia. Missionaries also used to prohibit students in mission schools from participating in the "bush schools" of the villages. These schools were secret initiation societies through which every tribal Liberian had to pass to become an accepted member of the society. A young person could hardly be blamed for not wanting to be "different" from all his friends.

Now, things are different. Bush schools are recognized as teaching some virtuous and useful things — absolute honesty and respect for elders; weaving, hunting, fishing, and planting. The strength of the old social order is admitted. The grandfather who comes to church is much more likely to bring his family with him than a younger man prepared to revolt against the established order. When Liberians wish to celebrate baptisms with feasts and parades, they do so even if missionaries may be uncomfortable because of their Western cultural inhibitions.

As a result, mission records in Liberia are showing the following: Gilikpaisu — 21 adults and 19 children baptized in a single service; Zomeh — 37 people preparing for baptism; Boheza — 96 decisions for baptism; Kiliwu — formerly six Christians, now 74 being instructed.

Variations of the people movement are being suggested for such widely divergent countries as Japan and

Argentina. In Japan attempts would be made to bring entire families (grandfather, father, son) — if not entire communities — into the church at one time. In Argentina, where congregations have traditionally been organized by inviting people from all over town to "come to church," multicongregational parishes are being suggested. Using the people movement concept of letting the church become a part of the people's culture, small groups would gather in various neighborhoods around whatever church activity appeals to them, or around a community problem that needs attention. One group might decide on Bible study, or another on education, a third on evangelistic services, a fourth on discussion.

No single pattern or time schedule would apply to every congregation of the parish. In time, regardless of the reason why the group began meeting, the gatherings might become the nucleus for a fully developed congregation. If so, the congregation would have arisen out of the people and their concerns — not imposed arbitrarily by a missionary.

In some senses the people movement is making some inroads into present American culture. Most churches are focusing ministries upon the various subcultures of society — apartment dwellers, businessmen, leisure-recreaction, jazz musicians, communes. Fortunately the focus upon such groups is usually part of a cross-section of ministry of a particular congregation. This prevents the small group idea from becoming an end in itself.

*A Lesson in Emotion*

About 3,000 people had gathered in the rather crude, arena-styled building in Santiago, Chile. Sixty percent of them were men, but many were women holding infants. In a row near the front, a distinguished man in his 60s with a small mustache began to cry. From time to time, his sobs became uncontrollable, and he dropped to his knees.

The preacher kept exhorting the listeners to persevere in the faith. From time to time he would shout to the congregation, "Did you like that?" The people would shout back, "Yes!"

These Pentecostal Christians like emotion. Manoel de Melo, healer, preacher, and president of a large church in Sao Paulo, Brazil, says that "traditional churches cannot attract the South American masses. The Brazilian temperament is different than that of the European. Our people like crowds and noise and emotion."

Brazilians and others in South America also like *Umbanda*, a form of spiritism that is a strange mixture of African and Indian tribal rites, superstition, and the veneration of saints that is so characteristic of Portuguese Catholicism. People from all walks of life—the military, the government, the poor—practice *Umbanda*, making wide use of incense, drums, blood, candles, and images. The first half of a typical *Umbanda* service focuses on "white magic," placating the good spirits and imploring healing and intercession. The second half evolves into "black magic," placing curses and hexes on those in disfavor.

Globs of wax and burned-out wicks can be seen daily along Rio's streets. On New Year's Eve, throngs of people push little boats containing candles out to sea, seeking the blessing of the goddess Yemanja. Tradition says that if the boats do not capsize in the waves, the new year will bring good fortune.

*Umbanda* is a "popular protest against all imported religious forms," declares Father Bonaventura Kloppenberg, Brazil's foremost authority on non-Christian religions. He notes that there are 764 Christian churches in Rio de Janeiro and vicinity, and 7,500 *Umbanda* centers.

The appeal of *Umbanda* and the temperament that likes crowds and emotion are the main reasons why

Pentecostalism is sweeping the continent. The transition from *Umbanda* to a Pentecostal type of worship is understandable. Both focus on emotion, healing, ecstasy, and participation. Both tend to be favored by the large lower class—many of them undereducated and economically marginal.

The other side of this fact is that the formality of the Roman Catholic Church and mainline Protestant churches do not appeal to these masses. The transition is too great, as evidenced by the fact that such worship is more attractive to the upper and middle classes.

The Pentecostals have great success among the poor—and there are a great many poor people in South America. Pentecostals understand because they *are* the poor. One pastor in Santiago, Chile, has only a first grade education. His congregation is made up of 300 "humble people" who have very little money.

Another lesson is that the Pentecostals usually train their clergy "from the people and among the people." Students are often attached to specific congregations to prepare for the ministry. The congregations also receive no subsidy from an outside board. Consequently they struggle to make ends meet.

Generally speaking, most Pentecostal church buildings in South America look makeshift and unfinished. Frequently they are constructed by volunteer workers from the congregation and decorated with their own art. The style of worship is their own. Often mainline Protestant churches in South America use Spanish translations of American and European songs, but Pentecostal music is usually that which is familiar to the people.

One Pentecostal congregation in Chile has three missionary "annexes." Another Pentecostal church in Santiago has a missionary in New York City. Most of all—and it is a strong reason for their success—they feel it is their business to preach the Gospel with vigor and individual fervor. Their growth underlines some of the fundamental characteristics of the church — evangelism, personal contact, worship in meaningful terms, and a large sense of commitment.

*Some of the Old Reasons*

The sign reading "Lutheran Radio Center" stands straight and tall against the blue African sky and the lush green shrubbery. Before long two blue and white buildings come into view down the road.

"Here we are," says Bert Mensah, my guide and the Lutheran Church in America's contribution to Tanzania's popular radio ministry. "When we first started, we set up our equipment in two-and-a-half rooms in a Bible school 30 miles from here," said Mensah. "Then we moved here in 1964. That's when I planted this tree."

Mensah may not have realized that his statements were symbolic. But like the station that outgrew the two-and-a-half rooms, and the tree that has grown 15 feet tall, the Lutheran Radio Center in Moshi has become one of the most influential arms of the Lutheran Church in Tanzania. In fact most observers credit it with being an important factor in the church's steady growth.

The Jamaica-born Mensah plays down his role in the center's operation. "I'm just a technician," he says. That is so, but every voice has to have its amplifier, and Bertram A. Mensah is the man who makes the church's word heard in Swahili every day for an hour and a half from the Congo to the Indian Ocean, and from Ethiopia to South Africa.

Along with a Tanzanian program director, Mensah and the center's 12-man staff produce tapes of music, drama, devotions, and religious instruction which are sent to the Radio Voice of the Gospel in Addis Ababa, Ethiopia. There the tapes are beamed over the Lutheran World Federation's powerful shortwave transmitter (31 meter band) to the lower third of the African continent. The Moshi studio is one of 14 in Asia, Africa, and the

Middle East which prepare tapes for transmission back to the producing areas.

Mensah's job is not easy. He had to design the studio in Moshi. When things break down, he fixes them. Hymns and other music in Swahili are not available, so twice a year he spends three or four weeks on safari, recording church choirs in Tanzania, Kenya, and Uganda. "Sometimes we record at three places in one day," he says. "And sometimes it takes us three days to drive to one place."

Worship services are not the only part of the center. Every Friday the program includes a Bible study that invites listeners to write for a correspondence course. Over the years nearly 10,000 letters have requested the course.

Pastor Amos Lyimo, until recently the center's program director, is convinced that "radio is one of the best missionary efforts in Africa today. Via radio we can enter non-Christian homes such as the homes of Muslims that we can't get into otherwise. If I go to preach in a town, only the Christians come. But radio reaches everybody.

"People like Christian radio," he continues. "They tell us that other stations have too many political programs or just cultural information. We have spiritual material and they like it.

"You must also remember that Tanzania does not have television. The government is soft-pedalling television because the country is so large. Instead they're pushing radio and encouraging every home to have one. They've even exempted radios from taxes. So people are buying radios to find out what is going on. Tanzanians listen first to TBC (Tanzania Broadcasting Company and the nation's only station), and second to the Radio Voice of the Gospel."

A general guideline for programs beamed by the Radio Voice of the Gospel is that 30 percent of the material can be directly evangelistic and 70 percent educational/cultural. This proportion is an attempt to bring the relevancy of the Gospel to bear on the whole of life. As a result, the station enjoys a particularly wide audience among the educated classes, including civil servants, teachers, professional people, and the military. "If St. Paul were alive today," boasts one station official, "he would be able to preach to more people in one hour on our station than he reached in his entire lifetime."

The International Lutheran Hour of The Lutheran Church—Missouri Synod also has far-reaching contacts through electronic evangelism. For example, Jesus Cuyo, a descendant of the Incas in Espinar, Peru, was listening to the Lutheran Hour in his home 13,000 feet up in the Andes. He wrote for some correspondence courses, decided he was a Lutheran, and organized a congregation. Now Cuyo has been commissioned as a Lutheran lay evangelist.

Although radio is one of the newer means of evangelism, it is one of a trio of rather standard efforts that the church has used for a number of years. Perhaps the oldest vehicle for the Gospel has been education. Virtually every mission in every part of the world has either a Sunday school or primary/secondary schools, or both.

The Lutheran Church—Missouri Synod has an enviable record in education in Hong Kong, for example, as do the Roman Catholics and the Church of Christ in China. The International School of The Lutheran Church —Missouri Synod in Hong Kong is open to students of all nationalities who can study in the English language.

Since the days of Father Heyer in India in 1842, the Lutheran Church in Andhra has developed an elementary school system. In 1959, when the church turned over its schools to the government, 800 such schools had been established.

In Tanzania, the statistics are even more striking. Where schools are established by the church, 95 percent of the youngsters from Lutheran homes attend, whereas the national average is about 50 percent. Church schools unknowingly educated Tanzania's future leaders. When the country became independent in 1961, the best jobs went to those who had the most education.

President Julius K. Nyerere attended a Roman Catholic school. Thomas Musa, a high-ranking member of the country's only political party, the Tanganyika Africa National Union (TANU), studied at a Lutheran primary school and is president of the church's Central Synod. Shadrock Ngowi, secretary of the church's northern diocese, is a regional chairman of TANU. Pastor Daniel Mfaume in Dar es Salaam is one of three clergymen who are members of the Tanzanian parliament.

But recently the government assumed control of the schools. "The property is a kind of gift to the government," says Joel Ngieyamu, executive secretary of the Evangelical Lutheran Church in Tanzania, "but the church's teachers, chapel, and religion classes will remain the same.

"Now we must explore other areas of education that the government is unable to handle," continues Ngieyamu, "such as schools for the physically handicapped or agricultural schools or trade schools." The time may have come for the church to start supplying teachers to the 1,900-student University of Tanzania. Also in effect is a "released time" plan for which Pastor Duane Nelson prepared a special curriculum and led seven teachers in instructing 1,117 junior and senior high school students in Dar es Salaam.

The point is that even though the schools may no longer belong to the churches in Tanzania or in India, education remains a basic vehicle for the spread of the Gospel. Through new arrangements the church continues to use education in aiding its growth.

The third of the familiar trio of evangelistic vehicles that the church has used is medical care. Again, in virtually every country clinics, hospitals, and mobile vans known as the "Jesus Car" are being used to express the church's concern to people who are suffering. By meeting people at this point of need, the church's larger message of healing and restoration to God has come into focus.

Martha Stoa, for example, is one of several missionaries sent out in recent years to implement a new medical strategy for dealing with leprosy. In Salur, India, she directed outpatient clinics and trained young Indians to serve as assistants.

"This is an exciting new day for leprosy work," she says. "Thanks to a sulfa drug discovered in the 1940s, the disease is now curable. We no longer have leper colonies where people are packed away for the rest of their lives. Now homes for leprosy sufferers can be turned into hospitals, and most leprosy patients can be treated on an out-patient basis. They can live at their homes. After all, leprosy isn't so contagious. You can't get it by casual contact.

"Education is helping change people's attitudes toward the disease," Martha continues, "even though the social pressures in the villages are still very real. As fear of the disease and ostracism grow less, we're getting more cases in the early stages, in which the leprosy can be arrested before the repulsive deformity occurs. If you went to a leprosy clinic today, you wouldn't be able to tell that most of the patients had the disease."

Martha Stoa knows that the ministry at Salur is a continuing example of the Gospel being borne to men on the wings of healing. In the same breath the work of Albert Schweitzer in Africa comes to mind – as does the ongoing medical treatment in church-sponsored clinics in Vietnam.

*Reaching Up to Christianity*

A single thread has run through these reasons for

church growth overseas. Whether it be radio evangelism, schools, medical centers, the rise of nationalism, political intrigue, sociological upheavals, people movements, or a love of emotion, there are strong indications that a certain hard-to-define socio-economic-political level has to be reached in a country before Christianity can make a dramatic impact.

Christianity presently tends to reach those who are reaching up from their former cultures. Certain minimal requirements in education, in understanding abstract concepts, in perspective of the wider world, and the vision of a fuller life seem to be prerequisites for receiving the Christian message.

One missionary family has lived and worked for 15 years among the Barabaig tribe on the shore of Lake Balangida in Tanzania, but has produced only 30 converts. The Barabaig live in *kraals* of sticks and straw and mud. The women wear brass rings around their necks and have circles burned around their eyes as beauty marks. The men have several wives and are crack hunters.

In most other areas of Tanzania, people have been more exposed to the outside world, and to sophistication, better health care, and familiarity with an economy other than agriculture. A strong case can be built that people need to reach such a level of socio-economic-political savvy before Christianity can flourish. The great majority of persons in Africa, Indonesia, and South American countries such as Brazil and Chile are reaching this level.

At this point they instinctively want to leave behind the vestiges of a past which they consider dark and undesirable. They want to move into the "new" day. When this happens, they discard their old customs — including their religion — because it reminds them too much of their recent past. Spiritism, animism, ancestor worship, tribal worship, and various codes which they followed in the past are now put aside. Some religion that is newer, more modern, and more sophisticated must take their place. Christianity with its Western, structured, and sophisticated flair is very appealing.

As an example of people clinging to that which is new — and downplaying their own past — consider a committee appointed by a congregation in Dar es Salaam, Tanzania, that was investigating changing the "white" Jesus who is painted over the altar into a "black" Jesus. The committee never altered the painting because the congregation later decided that it did not want to change the Jesus which the white man had brought them. Making Jesus black was returning them too quickly to their heritage.

Most missionaries are also encouraging Africanization of the Sunday worship through the use of traditional instruments and tunes. But most Africans prefer to use the hymns and liturgies of the missionaries. Traditional African forms are related in their minds to the days of poverty, ignorance, and domination which they want to leave behind. Perhaps the next generation will be far enough removed to look back appreciatively on their past, but the present generation lacks enough self-reliance to do so.

This observation does not deny the power of the Holy Spirit in bringing about conversions. But it does suggest that as there have always been opportune moments for the message of God to reach people, the opportune moment in these emerging countries is often influenced by a certain level of social, political, and economic understanding.

There is a corollary to this observation. As it seems necessary for people to reach a certain socio-economic-political level before Christianity can have a dramatic impact, so there appears to be another certain, hard-to-define socio-economic-political level that is a ceiling for the penetration of Christianity. High sophistication, scientific understanding, technical advancement, and mind-boggling communications seem to place religion — and Christianity in particular — in jeopardy. To some extent this phenomenon has occurred in Western Europe, Scandinavia, and America. Educated, sophisticated people in those countries are not sure that Christianity remains meaningful. So they drop out of the church.

In a real sense Christianity becomes a new superstition that these people are trying to leave behind as they climb above that upper ceiling where Christianity has its greatest impact. Note that the church is growing virtually everywhere in the world except in the United States, Western Europe, and Scandinavia. These countries have traditionally been the world's better developed areas. Expressions of Christianity as we have known them in America for nearly 400 years have reached the point where some think they must be radically altered if they are to be relevant and meaningful to modern man.

The lessons of history about such trends are familiar. The religion of Rome failed when the empire became too rich and self-assured. In the Old Testament Jeremiah warned the Israelites about their self-sufficiency and fatness. Proud Pharaoh in Egypt had his fall.

The role of church missions today is broader than just bringing the message of the Gospel to bear upon that middle ground of socio-economic-political status at which its hearers seem the most receptive. Its role is to find ways to penetrate the bottom level so that the message of Jesus goes into the most primitive areas, as well as to find the means for penetrating the top level so that the message is received and accepted by those who wish to leave it behind.

The message, of course, is that of Jesus the Christ. It is His love for them, their reconciliation to Him, and their relationship to their fellowmen. It is their faith as expressed in their private life and in communion with others in the fellowship of the church. It is the promise of new and abundant life here and hereafter.

In the words of the hymnwriter, it is the "old, old story." But because the story is now being told in these new settings and strategies for mission, the church desperately needs to take a fresh look at its worldwide role. A new day is dawning. For whatever else you may want to say about church missions overseas, it is certain that the practices of the future will be different from those of the past.

# FOR FURTHER READING

Beaver, R. Pierce. *From Missions to Mission*. New York: Association Press, 1964.

*Crossroads in Missions*. A multibook. Included are "The Missionary Nature of the Church," Johannes Blauw, "Missionary, Go Home!" James A. Scherer, "The Responsible Church and the Foreign Mission," Peter Beyerhaus and Henry Lefever, "On the Growing Edge of the Church," T. Watson Street, and "The Missionary Between the Times," R. Pierce Beaver. [1962-1968.] South Pasadena, Cal.: William Carey Library, 1971.

Lara-Braud, Jorge, ed. *Our Claim on the Future*. New York: Friendship Press, 1970.

McGavran, Donald. *Understanding Church Growth*. Grand Rapids, Mich.: Eerdmans, 1969.

Scherer, James A. *Mission and Unity in Lutheranism*. Philadelphia: Fortress Press, 1969.

Seltzer, S. and M. L. Stackhouse, eds. *The Death of Dialogue and Beyond*. New York: Friendship Press, 1970.

Thomas, Owen C., ed. *Attitudes Toward Other Religions*. New York: Harper & Row, 1969.

Winter, Ralph D. *The Twenty-Five Unbelievable Years 1945-1969*. South Pasadena, Cal.: William Carey Library, 1970.

*Chapter 1*

1. How can Americans develop more awareness of urban growth abroad? Travel? Pictures? Reading?

2. How can the church help governments, businesses, and tourists refrain from exploiting the resources of the developing cities — and from flaunting American wealth?

3. What help can Americans give in alerting new cities to the urban problems that plague the U. S.?

*Chapter 2*

1. Give other examples of American urban church life that have parallels with overseas church experiences.

2. Some local churches at home and abroad attempt to provide "something for everyone." This is called the "supermarket" approach. What are its advantages? What are the disadvantages, if any?

3. Why do Americans persist in regarding the achievements of overseas nations with surprise instead of admiration? Must the rest of the world have an exotic image before it can have meaning for us?

*Chapter 3*

1. Why have we failed to publicize the message of church growth overseas among American churchgoers — and therefore failed to use these successes as a boost for our own spirits?

2. The church is growing in the urban areas of the Third World. What does this suggest for our inner cities? Industrial areas?

*Chapter 4*

1. In what way can "tentmaking" ministries become a step toward more involvement between professional churchmen

95

and laymen at work? How can "tentmaking" be made a viable option in the American church?

2. Some say that crowded schedules, commuting time, and high-pressure jobs tend to prevent American laymen from having the time to engage in efforts similar to their counterparts overseas. Give suggestions for overcoming these difficulties.

3. In what respect can the lack of American lay involvement in churches become a denial of the priesthood of all believers?

*Chapter 5*

1. What is the necessary minimum of doctrinal unity before churches can engage in joint community projects? In joint worship?

2. The Lutheran Church — Missouri Synod and some other Christian bodies are wrestling with questions of interchurch cooperation. What is your feeling about it? The practice in your community?

3. Why is ecumenical work in the areas of social service and education more easily accomplished abroad than at home?

*Chapter 6*

1. Some church growth overseas indicates a close relationship between church and state. How can we better understand this phenomenon?

2. What political and sociological factors in North America seem to boost church growth? To suppress it?

3. What can main-line churches learn from the current surge of Pentecostalism in the world?

4. What examples of significant radio-television evangelism can you identify? Does mass media lend itself to personal decision-making? If so, how? If not, why not?

5. How can we help Christianity penetrate the upper "sociological-economic-political" level of American culture?